Dedicated to my wife Deanie (who inspires),
my gifted children Kirsten and Lars (who
wanted to be in the last book), my brother
Dino (who made it all possible), my mother
Candida (who thinks I can do anything),
and my father Anacleto, who, if he were here,
would still want an explanation as to why
I abandoned chemistry for design.

ISBN 0-946204-59-8
Library of Congress
Catalog Card Number 96-07796

Distributors to the trade in
the United States and Canada:
Watson-Guptill Publications
1515 Broadway,
New York, NY 10036

Distributed throughout
the rest of the world by:
Hearst Books International
1350 Avenue of the Americas
New York, NY 10019

Published by:
Madison Square Press
10 East 23rd Street
New York, NY 10010

Printed in Hong Kong

MAKING PEOPLE RESPOND

Design for Marketing & Communication

MADISON
SQUARE
PRESS

Contents

Acknowledgments   *5*

Foreword: Hal Riney on Art, Design, and Advertising   *6*

Introduction by Primo Angeli   *9*

Shelf-Competitive Products   *19*

How to Wrap Five Billion Apricots   *20*

Revolution and Evolution in the Beer Market   *28*

Launching into New Territory: From Premium Beer to Premium Soft Drink   *35*

A Tale of Three Confections   *38*

    The Story of the Big Name Candy   *39*

    The Case of the Unknown Company   *40*

    The Aloof Confection   *44*

Non-Shelf-Competitive Products   *47*

Designed for Sale and for Recognition After the Product Has Sold   *48*

Communicating to Engineers After They've Purchased Your Product   *49*

Creating Worldwide Imagery for Transaction Technology   *53*

Designing for a Captive Audience   *54*

Environmental Graphic Design   *59*

Packaging Buildings and Other Feats of Environmental Graphics   *60*

Instill a Sense of History and Create Functional Signage Through Environmental Graphics   *62*

The Permanence of Change   *68*

Posters   *73*

RapidAccess®   *87*

An Unorthodox Approach to Product Development   *88*

Designing Out of the Box   *92*

Events   *99*

San Francisco International Film Festival   *100*

Designing the "Look" of the 26th Olympiad in Atlanta   *104*

Gallery   *111*

The Absence of a Personal Style   *112*

Index   *143*

Acknowledgments

In any successful journey, the elements come together through planning and intuition. Some call it luck; others see it as anticipated goodness. We prefer the latter. This book is about the work of a group of creative individuals. As with commissioned musicians in an orchestra, these people play within a structured form. They also "compose." This creative performance is not too far removed from marketing design, where consumers, like an audience, demand clear emotional statements. Essentially, this orchestra consists of designers, sales people, directors, administrators, and managers, all working in an atmosphere of openness, where authorship and the creative process are shared. This team has a special mission: *Making people respond*. To these gifted individuals we are indebted.

I was a fine arts major in college. My grades were good enough, but after a year or two of carving zinc white from under my fingernails and washing charcoal off my shoes, I decided I might be a better peddler than a painter. So I switched to commercial art instead.

This decision was met with fairly universal disdain by my fellow students. True art, my more cultured cousins explained, belonged in the gallery or the studio. It had no place on the television screen or the cluttered shelves of the grocery store. Perhaps. But after thirty-seven years of working in advertising, I have concluded that my decision was right. I have no doubt that it would be a less interesting, less thoughtful and colorful world without the serious artist. But the tougher job is not adorning the walls and pedestals of the homes of the affluent. It is, to me anyway, the challenge of combining art with business, and attempting to bring style, beauty, good taste, and originality to many of those otherwise ordinary things that are a part of our everyday lives.

Traditional artists essentially serve themselves. Commercial artists – package, industrial, and graphic designers, creative staff at agencies, architects, filmmakers, illustrators, and photographers – are servants of others. Few of our employers share our passion for perfection, or even understand it. In the abstract, they may agree with our lofty arguments that we have an obligation not only to our clients, but also to the consumer and to society as a whole. Yet those same ideals are usually the first to fall prey to time, expediency, and the bottom line.

We insist, of course, that our art be original. Yet, to the great majority of our clients, originality implies risk. And business abhors risk. So the commercial artist's success or even survival demands perseverance, persuasion, and, especially, patience. I wonder what shape Rodin's sculptures might have taken had he submitted them to a focus group. Or what Monet might otherwise have painted if he had been served with a research study about people's indifference to water lilies.

The obstacles are endless, including the fact that the client's kid's favorite color is blue. Compounding the problem is that we have no absolute way of proving that what we believe and recommend is right. No computer can factor for us the proper proportions of psychology, aesthetics, and all the various marketing requirements that make up, for example, a package design. We can lean on, and learn from, research. But in the end the only absolute answer must come from the artist's own experience, taste, and intuition.

Fortunately, we are all arrogant enough to believe that if we like it, others will too. That is always our hope, our expectation, and, when it happens, our surprise. It is our reward for doing what we do. My art director partner, Jerry Andelin, and I have enjoyed working with Primo Angeli on the Henry Weinhard's project and other assignments as well. He has often helped us take what otherwise would be plain, faceless commodities and turn them into products that people use and like and admire. Primo is a serious artist, yet because of his extraordinary ability to satisfy both clients and customers, he is also a success in a complex and competitive commercial world, and has in motion a self-generating design philosophy and an extremely creative design group.

Do not, though, expect to see all of the firm's work in these pages. For every example that appears here, there were dozens or even hundreds of ideas discussed, dismissed, and discarded in favor of the one that seemed worth pursuing. The end result is an excellent, interesting, instructional book. Whether you are a designer yourself, a manager charged with a design project, or simply someone who is curious about the creative process, this strategic design organization will help you proceed a little faster, perhaps make fewer mistakes, and, I hope, find answers that are even better.

Hal Riney
Chief Executive Officer and Chairman
Hal Riney & Partners, San Francisco

INTRODUCTION

Primo Angeli

Is life a collection of packages? Instinctively, we label and sort everything we encounter into easily identifiable categories – "packages." From a commercial standpoint, any body of information with visual impact and a message could be a package – whether it is the suit you choose to wear to a job interview, the "Look" of the Olympic Games, or the graphics on your box of Quaker Oats. This is our way of establishing a visual language that allows us to organize and understand our external world. We expect these envelopes – these wrappings – to reflect truthfully what lies beneath. As shrewd American consumers, however, we are also trained to spot the discrepancies between form and content: the overpackaged person or product immediately strikes a dissonant chord.

In my 30 years as a graphic designer, I have become fully engaged with the dynamics and subtle intricacies of visual communication. Some of the basic principles of this medium are acquired through academic or intuitive effort, while others are learned only through extensive trial and error. To my mind, design for marketing and communication serves a special yet ultimately simple function: to sell a product or service. Aesthetic concerns are essential, but also serve as a means to an end. From the client's standpoint, our primary task is to communicate an idea and generate a response.

To that end, all forms of marketing communication can be most effective on a sensory and emotional level: designs must signal texture, temperature, aroma, and taste appeal. Credibility is paramount. Since consumers often see the package and the product as a single item, the relationship between the two must be seamless and consistent. A package – when it is important to the sale of the product – has to feel real. The graphics can be aesthetically interesting, but if the potential buyer has to stop and think about the surface design apart from the product, the purchase potential decreases. As in theater, when you are aware that an actor is acting, the spell is broken. Communication deteriorates to the level of mere decoration. Designers must be willing to remain objective and subsume their personal visual styles to create the most appropriate message for the product.

This field of ours is neither fine art nor wallpaper design, but the realm of commercial anticipation in which the surface graphics create the real value of the product; more often than not, we design in the realm of "frequent repeat purchase." A manufacturer, marketer, designer, or product will fail – it cannot survive – if the promise is inconsistent with the consumer's expectations. There is no advantage to visual deception – the consumer soon discovers the imbalance between the package and the product. If the consumer does not return after one purchase, the consequences can be severe, especially in a highly competitive free society open to a global market, whether the item in question is a boxed product, a packaged enterprise such as a shopping center, or a Web site. On the other hand, response will be limited if the graphics fail to stimulate the imagination. The consumer transfers a certain amount of expectation and fantasy to a product based on its presentation. It has been well documented that the same food product presented in two distinct packages, with one having less taste appeal, will elicit different taste responses.

Finally, marketing-design is a matter of context: knowing the product and its audience. First and foremost, before designing, the seasoned marketer will clearly position the product in the marketplace. The talent for discovering the unique and marketable characteristics of products and services is a designer's most valuable asset. For that reason, I believe creative teams should be composed of people with varied points of view. Diverse perspectives increase the occurrence of unforeseen inspirations that may sharpen or entirely change a design direction. Often, in the subconscious mind, an impulsive "hand" will inscribe visual renditions that the rational mind did not consider; had not been allowed to consider, because of time or other, self-imposed constraints. At that point, one should be willing to explore the new directions thus presented and abandon less intriguing design concepts regardless of whose brainchild they might have been.

In a partnership between marketing, design, and manufacturing, authorship and the creative process are shared so that ideas may flow freely. Professional pleasure comes from playing in a cooperative atmosphere that engenders openness, constructive criticism, and a contagious desire to assist each other in making motivational pictures. It is this attitude that makes anything possible.

Immersed in a conversation at the breakfast table, I reach for a glass of milk and unwittingly find a glass of tomato juice. I drink from it, anticipating the taste of milk. A sharp acid taste overpowers my taste buds: "Sour milk!" The mix-up sets in motion a confusion of thought and taste until I realize that what I think I am tasting is completely different from what my taste buds tell me I am tasting. Signals. How often, in more subtle and unconscious ways, do we design mixed signals into a message, and into our communications in general?

Material Matrimony

This kind of dissonance is obviously not the reaction we want consumers to experience when they confront a brand or open a package. As consumers, we have an intuitive feeling for the compatibility between packaging materials and the products they contain. The external packaging triggers a sense of anticipation of what will be found inside. Choosing materials that complement rather than clash with a product goes a long way toward fulfilling those expectations. We respond positively to certain combinations, such as pewter and beer, silver and cream, oil and tin. Other combinations clash: wine in a can, beer in a carton. Yet hard and fast rules are made to be broken. Materials by their very nature tend to create a certain reaction. Translucent sheets used in a brochure cause the reader to slow down and savor the design. Newsprint, a basic, functional medium for immediate use and recycling, has the opposite effect. Low-priced mass-produced snack foods should also be readily accessible, the wrapping making a crisp noise as it is torn open and the product is consumed. For these products, overpackaging is a wasteful and confusing signal that inhibits purchase. At the other extreme are premium chocolate manufacturers such as Godiva and Harden & Huyse, who do not create an exquisite product only to wrap it in a paper bag. This product is a luxury and should be presented as such.

Packaging materials must minimize the distance – and dissonance – between the consumer's anticipation of the product and what is inside the package. This integration signals a wholeness to the product so that there is no hesitation, no confusion, just a harmony between what is seen, anticipated, taken, and repeated. Ideally, it should be a consistent message to consumers in a market of past and repeat purchases.

Sense Appeal

An entire book could focus on the importance of communication and the senses. Until there is time and energy for us to devote to such a project, we defer to some exceptional works that already exist, such as Diane Ackerman's *A Natural History of the Senses*. Taste, touch, sight, scent, sound, and that elusive sixth sense, intuition, are the tools on which designers depend. Because they are for human consumption, food and beverages top the list of products that require the full expression of all the senses.

Food and beverages are more challenging to package than other products because they must "taste" and feel right visually. They must also inform you of their effects: slim you down, fatten you up, keep you healthy. Yet whether selling Nestlé chocolate, Adobe software, or Apple computers, packaged communication is "beeping" on a sensory level. Even hardware products should have sex appeal, a voluptuousness that makes them ergonomically palatable or that suggests "deliciousness": these beautiful forms in machinery and tools demand appreciation. Cosmetics can become almost edible.

A food package should immediately communicate the nature of its contents: rich or bland, sweet or sour. Colors instantly translate these sensory messages. When indicating color for Italian tomato paste, reds, yellows, and greens refer to the fresh ingredients inside. Pink carries with it a certain sweetness. Gold and silver are commonly used with chocolate because they contrast with and complement it. The translucence of wax paper conjures the tactile sense and taste of beeswax, an edible preservative. But these are examples of past usage and not to be taken as rules. A case-by-case consideration is necessary for appropriate communication.

The use of imagery says something about a product; more important, it triggers an emotional response with the recipient. The scents of flowers, eucalyptus, pine, earth, and thousands of other aromas call up our shared experiences as consumers; these smells have a common context within our lives. There is also the thermal element to consider – whether something is visually hot or cold, for instance, in taste expectation. Automatically, these are some of the vital graphic cues, besides the literal printed word, on which a designer depends. In this way, consumers can individualize a product and establish a common visual language. Perhaps the greatest sense a designer has to develop is intuition. Despite all the marketing research in the universe, it eventually comes down to the intuition of a designer, marketer, or manufacturer: someone has a feeling about something, and, although rarely admitted, that is often the motivation for action. An intuition can move mountains of logic into an eloquent rationale.

The Word
The design process often begins with writing, either a concise brief that accurately positions a product or a working title that suggests a certain attitude. Words not only convey information; they create texture and tone as well. As Mark Twain said, "The difference between the right word and the almost right word is the difference between lightning and a lightning bug."

Although we are first and foremost a design consultancy, a growing number of clients approach us as a resource for naming. Great names are the result of a number of complex characteristics in combination. They are easy to read, generally easy to pronounce, and easy to remember because they project a personality. More than mere descriptors, product names and even working titles should evoke emotion, not feel contrived. Without sensitivity and appropriateness to the product, an improper name becomes a constant barrier. Then there are those instances when a name sounds fantastic but does not work typographically: there are too many characters, or the word contains an awkward series of letters that pose visual hurdles. These concerns usually surface through the design process. Names have to perform when they are seen as well as when they are spoken. Beyond the name itself lie deeper layers of communication. Storytelling plays a dynamic role, whether dealing with product descriptors, vital information, or overall image. We keep running checklists of qualities that make products unique, and often use them to remind clients of distinctions they may have overlooked. A phrase such as "Original Recipe" or "Draft Style Head" can say a lot about a product. At other times a sentence or an entire paragraph may be necessary.

In addition to our creative staff, we brainstorm with copywriting consultants worldwide to supplement our research. Because developing names and copy for international regions requires specific cultural and linguistic expertise, we always consult foreign-language and -market specialists when designing products to be sold outside the United States.

Ultimately, we use every tool at our disposal to get the correct message across. The words we choose must be visually interesting, they must be real and true to the product or service, and most important, they must be well integrated with the visual design, and must endure in the marketplace.

Computer technology is transforming our society in ways as radical as the advent of movable type, the harnessing of electricity, or the invention of fiber optics. These changes signal the death of one era and the birth of a new one. I have never wanted to be a lifetime member of any style, tool, or era, so the computer revolution and cyberspace do not give me vertigo. Having realized that we can do nothing to turn back the clock, we are finding numerous ways to use new technology to work more effectively and efficiently.

Perhaps in the future we will evolve beyond typography to an even more visual, nonverbal world communicating mental projections, where one grunt is worth a thousand words. David Carson's excellent work at *Ray Gun* magazine explored new forms in which typography is featured as a visual medium meshed into pictorial configurations that clearly communicate to a dif-

Building Bridges and Burning Technology

ferent world of human receptors. His graphics represent new forms in finessing printed communication, often with a jackhammer sensitivity, but commanding the viewer's attention and making waves in our field of design.

What will interactive technology do to the designer and the package in the short run? Not a lot. But in the long run, in the virtual shopping mall – the world of on-line marketing in which graphics are so compelling that you will place orders right off your display panel – advertising and packaging design will merge. As values change and delivery systems are revolutionized, packaging as we know it will certainly become obsolete.

For me – an animal still firmly planted in the realm of the senses, the emotions, the handshake, and the handmade – it is a real challenge to achieve a smooth link between present and future. On the one hand, I have the uncomfortable feeling that we are experiencing the end of the human being as we know him/her/it: our innate activities, instincts, and abilities will succumb to digital devices (new, improved tentacles?). Yet I am intrigued by the ways in which technology will incite alternative forms of communication. Solace as well as inspiration are contained in this quote from St. John, which I keep on my desk: "I am not made or unmade by the things that happen to me but by my reaction to them." New models. New bridges. New horizons.

Primo Angeli

SHELF-COMPETITIVE PRODUCTS

One of my favorite books on design is graphic designer Hideyuki Oka's *How to Wrap Five Eggs*, a celebration of traditional Japanese packaging. The author fell in love with the natural materials – rice straw, paper, ceramic pots and bottles, wooden boxes – that were used for packaging in his country before the rise of mass manufacturing. In the book's introduction, Mr. Oka asks, "If the craftsmen and 'designers' of old Japan could create beauty with their materials, are we to accept defeat when faced with ours?" This question offers great insight into the challenge we faced when designing a package for California-based dried-fruit producer, Mariani Packing Company. Instead of being asked to wrap five eggs, however, we were charged with packaging five billion apricots, as well as 30 other product categories. Obviously, we had to research the functional materials of modern mass marketing. The packaging we designed combined acts of looking forward and of looking back – blending a sense of tradition with new technology to arrive at an elegant and effective solution. Sometimes an exceptional product will have such mundane packaging that its graphic presentation needs a dramatic upgrade. For a communications and marketing designer, this

Sometimes the product deserves a far better package than the one it has.

situation is ideal. Build expectations too much, and you risk disappointing the consumer. If the manufacturer is asking a premium, and your graphic identity lives up to it, the product had better perform as well.

Mariani Packing Company is a century-old family-owned business in San Jose, California, specializing in over 30 different dried-fruit products. Unlike most of its competitors, the company takes many extra steps when processing the fruit, an effort that translates into quality. Despite having a superior product, Mariani was awash in a sea of dried-fruit products from such corporate giants as Sunsweet, Dole, and Del Monte. Mariani's bags were often found tossed into bins or lying flat on the shelf, with no ability to communicate the quality of the product inside.

Recognizing enormous potential to increase the company's share of the market, owner Mark Mariani and newly-hired marketing director Mark Bagley came to us in 1992 to revamp the entire brand profile. Although Mariani's products cost more to process and were considered better than the competing products in the market, the existing identity and packaging exhibited a "just off the farm" look, an image that had a certain naïve charm but didn't convey a sense of consistency. The straightforward design brief required that we create a proprietary look and a distinctive taste appeal. We set out to do something natural, delicious, and bold.

The Brand Mark: The Starting Point

An obvious starting point was the trade name, Mariani: a red scribble across the package top that gave the impression of an unclear private label. For this brand we created a lettering style that was larger and easier to read. By embellishing the lettering with a shadow and gold highlights, it became richer and more three-dimensional. The name now had authority. Initially, we were looking to enrich this new brand mark with an illustration of assorted fruits. Soon we realized that this idea didn't accurately represent all of Mariani's products. The next question was, "What else would enhance the value of this brand?" Mariani being a family operation, we considered the founder's endorsement. By using a stylized image of P. A. Mariani, we could let people know that Mariani is not a faceless corporate operation but a family concern: someone was watching the store. None of the competitors could make a similar claim. P. A. Mariani's signature completed this graphic distinction.

Package Comps and Roughs

From the logo we launched into the actual package, creating three different approaches. One emerged as the obvious winner. The initial concept placed the Mariani logo straight across the top of the package with a product-identification banner arching from top to bottom. Normally, it is the brand logo that says, "Look at me!" But in this particular case, we incorporated the brand and the arched product designator into a single design element, creating a dynamic focal point to command consumer attention.

Zip Lock Top

Not only is the package resealable to protect the freshness of the product, it also boasts the value-added quality of being reusable.

Orange Crate Graphics

In addition to a see-through window, we chose to portray the fruits in the context in which they're grown. San Francisco air-brush artist Robert Evans created illustrations of the fruit on the tree in a style described as "orange crate graphics." The combination of the dynamic logo and banner design, the luscious illustrations, the intricately textured package, and the visible high-quality dried fruit resulted in an impact the product alone could not begin to approach. The whole had transcended the sum of its parts. Suddenly there was texture, aroma, freshness, and heightened taste appeal.

Mariani's investment in converting to our new packaging solution was considerable, but the outcome was most impressive. By transforming its product line to a much-deserved premium

status, distribution expanded into previously untapped markets, such as drug and discount chains and the growing club stores. In the first year after the introduction of the new packaging, Mariani's sales were up 50%; by the end of the second year, total sales had doubled. There was no increase in advertising and no reformulation of the product. This success was in large part attributable to the package.

The Stand-Up Pouch

Another piece of the puzzle required designing a structure that would allow the product to sit properly on the shelf, enabling our graphic

treatments to form an immediate block of power billboarding. After some initial attempts, Mark Bagley offered a possible solution. He had seen Japanese packaging that made use of gusseted bags – packages with a preformed bottom or floor that allows them to stand up. We added a resealable feature to protect the freshness of the product. While we were extremely excited about this prospective package, we were concerned that its expense might prove

prohibitive. After great deliberation, Mark Mariani took a step into the unknown, hoping that, with such a delicious look, the business would follow. He trusted his instinct that consumers would respond to quality. A year later, the new packaging system at Mariani's San Jose facility was up and running, relying on a combination of American and Japanese technology to produce the packages. In two years, sales had doubled.

For many years, Heileman's Old Style beer had been the number one brand name in Chicago, the United States' third largest beer market. But when Midwestern giants Miller Brewing Company and Anheuser-Busch began to outspend Heileman on television ads and endorsements by a factor of ten to one, sales took a predictable slide. Worse yet, the Windy City's young drinkers were not taking to Heileman's newest products, Light and Dry. Launched in 1980 and 1988, respectively, these new beers were performing poorly, with little or no support from lackluster package designs. The Heileman brief was twofold, requiring that each product communicate to a different customer while sharing a common graphic unity. Old Style was a recognized brand that needed to be revitalized. Heileman Light and Dry represented the new categories of light, high-quality beers aimed at younger audiences. All fell under the broader category of "literal branding," in which the design shouts its message to consumers.

Understanding the positioning – knowing exactly what the customer anticipated from each beer – was the critical first step. Thorough market research showed that loyal Old Style drinkers would probably not accept a radical packaging and image change. On the other hand, focus groups considered the current Light packaging to be generic and unappealing. All ages agreed that the Dry packaging failed to promise a unique, fulfilling beer-drinking experience. The direction became clear: Old Style required evolutionary changes, while Light and Dry needed drastic, revolutionary design work. Each of the three beers had its own audience: older, younger, and a mixture of the two.

Problem: Communicate three different types of beer to three different audiences, all under the same brand.

Old Style Lager

The changes to the Old Style packaging came in the form of subtle embellishments: the shield was cleaned up and sharpened; a drop shadow added dimension to the ribbon. By centering the product identifier and using rich details around the type, we strengthened the Old Style identifier. On top of all this increased substance, we convinced the client to reintroduce the name Heileman, which had been omitted from the previous can design. This name represented a founder – and a German brewer at that. Taking advantage of the power of heritage only served to amplify the authenticity and credibility of the brand. From a marketing standpoint, it made no difference that the Heileman family name was unknown to consumers. What mattered, we argued, was that a family name – especially a strong German name – would lend authenticity, tradition, and authority to the rather generic Old Style brand identity.

Premium Light Beer

In contrast to the well-established Old Style brand, Light was in need of a serious redesign. "Light" appeared so innocuously on the can that it made the beer seem like a private label, with no authority. Our question was, "How can we make this appeal to younger drinkers?" We decided on two primary directions: to put "Light" center stage, and to keep the design fresh, dynamic, and proprietary. The primary message was a feeling of lightness, captured in part by silver and white. The Heileman shield became an endorsement, a kiss on the top of the can. Since "cold" always surfaced as the top taste-appeal attribute in consumer tests, we created a "gulpable," refreshing look – no more old-fashioned, pot-bellied European beer image, not for this audience.

While a paper label on a bottle allows for several color variations, an aluminum can restricts the designer to four colors (more would drive up the unit cost, making the beer unacceptably expensive). The thin "stay away" lines prohibit overlapping colors. While a tonal change might be effected with a screen, this process often turns out coarse and washed out; recent printing technology is improving, however, and at reasonable cost. To add dimension and dynamics, we used cross-hatch lines to create tonal effects, such as shading.

Premium Dry Beer

Heileman's Dry had a different positioning: a higher alcohol beer with no aftertaste. Our design solution split the difference between the other two approaches: we gave "Dry" and "Old Style" roughly equal importance on the can. Usually it is best not to divide the brand name and product name because it jeopardizes the focal point. In this case we felt it was appropriate. Flourishes and decorations around the shield – also featured on the Light can – became more prominent on the Dry. We added gold striping that starts heavy at the bottom and tapers off toward the top. The gold lines allow the silver in the background to shine through, creating a synergistic relationship between the two colors. This technique delivered a richer taste and more substance to the Old Style Premium Dry, as opposed to the lighter taste and faster drink capability of the Premium Light.

Secondary Packaging

Secondary packaging plays an essential role in beer sales in the United States, where most beer is consumed at home. The opposite is true in Ireland and England, where social custom favors drinking in pubs. As drunk driving laws and random breath testing become more common throughout Northern Europe, however, visual presentation of packaging and products will no doubt respond accordingly.

Problem: Communicate three different styles of beer to the same consumer group, all under the same brand.

We've created a number of beer identities over the years, from mainstream to super premiums to microbreweries. This field is both an art and a science. A new generation of beer drinkers has brought changes in both tastes and consumption patterns that make the task challenging and exciting. The key, as always, is understanding beyond a shadow of a doubt the attributes of the product as well as its marketing position – will it be the parent for other beers, or simply a line extension? Only then can you begin to create the product's personality.

The case of Henry Weinhard's super-premium beers offers an excellent counterpoint to the G. Heileman case. San Francisco–based advertising maven Hal Riney called us to design the original packaging for this beer when the line was introduced in 1976. Subsequently the company was purchased by Pabst, which later sold it to G. Heileman Brewing Company. Rather than producing three separate products to appeal to as many distinct audiences, Portland-based Henry Weinhard's three Private Reserve beers all targeted the same upscale consumer.

Group Identity, Individual Expression

All three labels originate from the same graphic family, yet each communicates its own identity. Private Reserve Dark expresses a heavier, more substantial image while Light Beer's silver label captures the quality of effervescence. Here the same design offers variety to a core group of consumers, achieving a contemporary application of traditional graphic elements.

Historic Coincidence

We explored traditional imagery as part of the research process for the Henry Weinhard's logo. After we presented our logo, Hal Riney showed us an antique glass bearing an uncannily similar emblem: an eagle in the center with a "Henry Weinhard's" banner above.

Henry Weinhard's

ROOT BEER

PREMIUM

Draught Style Head

A gourmet Root Beer, hand finished with only the highest quality ingredients including sassafras, honey and vanilla.

6-12 FL. OZ. BOTTLES

When Jack Hanzlovic of G. Heileman Brewing Company called about a hot new product from Henry Weinhard's, he presented an exciting but complex mission: root beer! With a line extension into handcrafted, quality soft drinks, the Chicago-based beer company was stepping into new territory. It was essential to Heileman's management that consumers continue to respect the established Henry Weinhard's premium beer products while appreciating and purchasing this new, high-end root beer. The association of the Weinhard name with a yeasty beer taste could potentially clash with a consumer's anticipation of a sweet, creamy soda. Our challenge was to take advantage of Henry Weinhard's reputation for quality to create upscale imagery for the new root beer. The positioning statement called for an adult-oriented soft drink with a sense of tradition and authenticity. This was indeed a *gourmet* root beer with a special taste.

Although there was no existing original packaging, the product itself was drawn from an original Henry Weinhard's recipe that harked back to the "Great Dry Spell," the days of Prohibition. In order to produce "great graphics," it is imperative that you have a good product and a good client capable of making decisions. This was the case with Heileman. Root beer is as American an institution as hamburgers and hot dogs. Heileman's journey into the past – based on an old product recipe – has opened the door to the future: handcrafted soft drinks could revolutionize the beverage industry. Heileman and other companies are sure to delve more deeply into these frontiers, developing diversified lines of gourmet and mainstream products to meet new consumer demands.

The Consumer's Opinion

The selection of a beer bottle for this soft drink product presents a small procedural matter worthy of mention. During our research, we considered many different glass containers and ultimately chose a long-necked brown beer bottle, which might have visually implied "beer" rather than "root beer." (Taste buds don't appreciate receiving confusing signals sent to the brain from the eyes.) We realized the potential discrepancy but nevertheless decided to trust our strong intuitions. In early market testing, consumers ruled out the traditional long-necked beer bottle, but we pursued the idea anyway. The focus group had judged a bottle without final graphics on it, a practice I have always questioned because, without a realistic prototype, the consumer is vulnerable: emotional graphic imagery can change everything. We ignored the premature consumer opinion and used the bottle in an alternate design – which surfaced as the best one. Heileman went along and earned its entire year's sales projections in the first quarter. Obviously, consumers now like the bottle.

Graphic Harmony

After much experimentation, we chose to use the product identifier – "Root Beer" – as the prominent graphic feature on the label, a departure from the usual route of emphasizing a well-known brand over the product identifier. The Weinhard name was strongly associated with beer; if "Root Beer" had appeared smaller than the Weinhard name on the label, it might not have sent a strong enough visual signal about what the product really was. As it turned out, all elements were in perfect balance. The combination of an extra bold outline around the letters of the words "Root Beer," enhanced by embossed detailing, gave the impression of thickness and substance. Our maroon and cream imagery captured a richness that, when impressed on a clear film label, seemed to have been printed on the glass. The flavor, sweetness, carbonation, and dark color were perfectly complemented by the brown, long-necked glass bottle. This was one instance when the angels really smiled on us. Everything flowed into one, rich, and enticing entity.

Authentic Details

Relying on a few key elements from the Weinhard's beer packaging that we introduced 20 years ago, a natural imagery surfaced. One of the main departures from the Private Reserve beer label was the introduction of a picture of Mr. Henry Weinhard himself, surrounded by wooden barrels. The illustrations are reminiscent of old steel-line engravings; we fine-tuned the design to recall the Prohibition Era of the '20s.

It can't be stressed enough that in order to produce great graphics, you have to have a good product and a good client capable of making decisions.

What does it take to design something "sweet"? Colors with particular taste appeal? Graphics that signal immediacy or preciousness? Unwrapped, a confectionery product stands naked, with no means to communicate to consumers in a shelf-competitive environment; the only way to appreciate the qualities of an unwrapped chocolate or candy is to taste it. The bottom line is that the graphics and packaging have to offer an honest representation of the product: is it intended to be devoured or savored? Once the ultimate positioning of the product is certain, the design process can begin. In the following section, we detail three different confections, each with a distinct long-range graphic solution.

The Story of the Big Name Candy

38

If your product has the track record of a candy bar like Butterfinger, you don't want to mess around too much with a good thing. After Nestlé purchased Butterfinger from R.J. Nabisco, it approached us with the task of refining the product graphics. Its main concern was maintaining the mass appeal of its newly acquired product. Nestlé also wanted to enhance the product's image by adding a Nestlé endorsement that would capitalize on the company's worldwide reputation for quality but not significantly impose on Butterfinger's brand equity. The graphics would be used in primary packages as well as on display trays and other point-of-sale materials.

As you've seen throughout this book, evolutionary changes are often the appropriate course of action to take with a product that is already widely popular and vital in the marketplace. Even at this point, however, slight modifications are considered significant. We explore design possibilities as thoroughly and carefully as if we were introducing a brand new product. In this case, the Nestlé name became a subtle but valuable graphic endorsement without jeopardizing the traditional appeal of its famous image.

Regardless of the temptation, the visual solutions of any new parent company must always respect and reflect the existing identity of a product — unless that image is so eroded that it requires a major overhaul. This has a lot to do with that invaluable ability to get inside the shoes of consumers and understand how they perceive the product. Here, Butterfinger gained a new last name, one that will surely sustain momentum in an industry where the competition can be anything but sweet tempered.

The Case of the Unknown Company

Secret Identity

Despite its range of nearly 60 different confections, Brown & Haley lacked an immediately recognizable brand identity. To the right are some of the company's previous packages, all with different graphic treatments.

We call this story "The Case of the Unknown Company" because, when Brown & Haley approached us in 1993 to develop a program for its branding and packaging, the company faced an unusual dilemma. Although it had been in business since 1912, and sold a range of nearly 60 different products, it was known primarily for its world-famous Almond Roca. This unique confection features a sweet, crisp, buttercrunch cloaked in a layer of chocolate and almond shavings. Just as distinctive as this delectable confection is the Almond Roca package, a striking pink box that has earned Brown & Haley generations of loyal customers. These graphics, however, did little to promote the brand name.

Without the power of a unifying, single brand entity, Brown & Haley's other products seemed as though they were marketed by different companies. While the company couldn't afford to advertise each one of its 60 products individually, it couldn't capitalize on its brand equity either. The name had simply been buried for too long. Still, Brown & Haley wanted to broaden the awareness of its company name and take advantage of a long, successful tradition.

What's in a Name?

For decades, Almond Roca spoke louder in the marketplace than the Brown & Haley brand name itself. We gave the brand name a strong sense of identity without compromising the enormously popular Almond Roca image. The company's other product lines immediately benefited.

BROWN & HALEY

SINCE 1912

ALMONDROCA

Our first objective was to take this distinctive, authoritative name, Brown & Haley, and give it personality and presence so that it would be recognized as a brand. Until then it had been inconsistently applied to products – sometimes as the dominant graphic, sometimes as a mere endorsement; at other times it was nearly nonexistent. As we redesigned the logotype, trademark, and product packaging, our focus was on unifying the family of products underneath the Brown & Haley name. In the end, we found that although we were not personally fond of pink, we couldn't radically redesign the Almond Roca package: the risk of disappointing consumers was too great. However, by establishing the prominence of the Brown & Haley brand name on the Almond Roca package as well as on other products, we set in motion the process of transferring some of Almond Roca's popularity over to the rest of the lines. Instead of whispering "Brown & Haley" and shouting "Almond Roca," the famous confection found its name. And with that balanced approach, we were able to set the stage for Brown & Haley to be the primary carrier of the brand imagery. This solution created a positive forward trajectory – and increased the value of the corporation.

Establishing a Name

*With the Brown & Haley brand name
clearly and consistently positioned
throughout all its product lines,
the company surfaced as an entity.*

The Aloof Confection

Sweet dreams can mean different things to different people. For Anthony and Claude Hardenne, two adventurous brothers from Saskatchewan, sweet dreams took on a literal meaning. The Hardennes envisioned a future as entrepreneurs in the confectionery business, where they wanted to be known for selling the world's finest chocolates.

Throughout the course of their many international excursions, the Hardenne brothers always went to great lengths to learn about chocolate. By visiting most of the world's major chocolate manufacturers, they became well versed in the business and its techniques and recipes. When the time finally arrived for them to launch their Saskatchewan-based world-class chocolate company, they had done a great deal of homework. The company, Harden & Huyse (the brothers simplified the Hardenne name by dropping the final "ne"), then approached us for branding and packaging. The position statement clearly stated that Harden & Huyse would compete head on with such international heavyweights as Godiva, Lindt, and others that sold super-premium chocolates throughout North America and Canada.

HARDEN & HUYSE

&

CHOCOLATES

Although an infinite variety of design solutions and possibilities existed, there was, really, only one approach to the project. We weren't just branding and packaging something chocolate or sweet, but something exquisite. Harden & Huyse used only the finest (and very expensive) ingredients in its chocolates. It was imperative that the graphics reflect this luxuriousness.

As the design unfolded, we developed an abstract, fluid pattern with swirls and gradations of colors that suggests a melting together of cream and chocolate. The logotype, printed in gold and surrounded by an embossed rectangular box, gives the impression of a label placed on the very finest wrapping paper. Essentially a typographic design, it relies on simplicity and the unusual name, Harden & Huyse, for eccentricity and uniqueness.

We intentionally kept the graphics devoid of any mainstream product-photography taste appeal, creating a package that could hold something precious: perhaps chocolate, perhaps fine Italian silk stockings. How would one immediately know? This desirable ambiguity is effective within the context of the confectionery shelf-sales environment, where the product gains its identity from the other products that surround and compete with it. Our design has imbued Harden & Huyse with the high-end imagery of marked sophistication. We didn't wish to push the "commercial envelope" on this one. And it works.

NON-SHELF-COMPETITIVE PRODUCTS

Often a consumer will not recognize a billboard advertisement for a certain brand of automobile until he or she owns that car or truck: until you have a Ford, you won't necessarily notice a Ford billboard. After the purchase, there is a sense of pride and confirmation in seeing the brand name. In this instance, the billboard functions not as primary information but as a means of building a brand reputation over time.

This same logic applies to such packaged products as high-end software programs not sold in a shelf-competitive environment. Whereas food and beverage items are "frequent repeat purchase" products, these non-shelf-competitive products are often expensive commercial items not purchased by the same consumer on a weekly jaunt to a local store. While the product must be easily located in stores, it must also visually reinforce the software's high value and continue to promote it in the workplace. Also falling into this category are any number of reusable point-of-purchase items, from shopping bags to shoe boxes.

When computer systems managers purchase expensive and essential software programs, it is important to reassure them that they are receiving a high-quality, cutting-edge product. The "mark" must be easily identifiable. It should capture – both abstractly and directly – the essence of the product. Ultimately, the packaging will end up on a shelf as a case for the software's operating manuals, thus serving as a continual reminder of the crucial function the software plays within the overall industry. When it comes to designing packages for high-end software systems, there is a great temptation to use extravagant materials. Why not explore wood, metal, or glass to create the longest lasting impact? After all, we are striving to communicate the essential value of the product long after purchase. But overpackaging is a waste of materials and budgets – cardboard and paper can accomplish the same mission just as effectively. The outdated "glitz deco" design mindset sends a poor signal to consumers and the public at large, even if the client can afford the additional expense. Now more than ever in global history, there is good reason to avoid design stylists and decorators who allow personal artistic expression to overshadow effective communication and merchandising in a time of ecological concern for survival. It can be counterproductive to both the planet and the manufacturer.

David Galli, Communications Director for XILINX, knew of our reputation for "consumer-friendly packages" when he approached us in 1991 to position and package the company's newest software development system, XACT 4000. Although XACT 4000 would not be shelf-competitive, he realized that the engineers for whom the product was targeted would respond well to a stimulating packaging approach. XILINX, based in San Jose, is the world's largest supplier of CMOS programmable digital logic – the proverbial "glue" that connects the microprocessor to the memory in a computer system. A software producer known for innovation, it designs programs that assist developers of telecommunications products, medical

Communicating to Engineers After They've Purchased Your Product

instrumentation, industrial controls, and robotics. XACT 4000 represented a huge breakthrough for engineers who design high-density semiconductor circuitry. It enabled them to use the computer to design the circuitry as well as to test and fine-tune their inventions, thus reducing development time by months and saving the money, time, and effort typically expended in producing and testing prototypes.

We devised dozens of ways to communicate XACT 4000's primary message, and came up with symbolism that visually portrays the product's function. Since we were designing for a high-tech company, we decided to present our ideas to the client on a Macintosh computer at XILINX headquarters, where we showed each design alternative in the context of the product's objectives and positioning. Using the computer, we were able to fine-tune the graphics right there in the conference room.

We made this computer presentation (a gesture greatly appreciated by the client) at a time when Macintosh was not yet in the mainstream for designers. It went off beautifully, even though we had forgotten to bring the power cord for the computer – a detail that exposes our vulnerability to the technologies on which we have become so dependent. Luckily, a jury-rigged connector got us into action. XACT 4000 went on to become the company's top revenue-generating product.

Symbols

The concept that was ultimately chosen offered a layered message to software users. The image of the computer screen, the ruled yellow paper airplane, the engineer, designer, manufacturer, the illusion of deep space – all were carefully chosen intimations and symbols portraying traditional pencil-and-paper methods encountering and interacting with the newer tools of information and communication.
Less time, more space.
Friendly.

Omnihost™

Ever wonder how the swipe of a credit card can instantaneously process transactions? Automated transaction technology is the essence of Omnihost, a software program created by Verifone, Inc., a Silicon Valley firm with a reputation for excellent point-of-sale systems products. Omnihost is the operating system that processes credit ratings after a card has passed through a sensor. Three different product categories target distinct groups of value-added retailers: single stores, shopping centers, and national retail chains. At the time of our design, the software packages cost $10,000, $20,000, and $30,000, respectively.

With the introduction of Omnihost, Verifone was positioned to supply complete transaction automation systems as a single-source vendor. There was virtually no competition. Even though the product wouldn't be distributed at retail, we felt the packaging should feature dynamic graphics that command attention in the workplace. For the visual identity, we created a simple expression of form and function. Integrated into the "O" of the Omnihost name are two dominant graphic symbols: a sphere representing the globe and the world marketplace and, circling the planet-like sphere, a ring suggesting velocity and cutting-edge technology. The combined effect of the two concepts transcends the impact of each element alone. Finally, three different colors – red, yellow, and blue – distinguish the product categories.

Color Coding

Since the Omnihost line includes three different products aimed at distinct target retailers, we gave each product its own color.

Designing for a
Captive Audience

You are in a hotel bathroom – not exactly trapped, but a captive audience nevertheless. Except for a few items you brought along in your travel kit, the personal products you use – soap, shampoo, lotion – are not of your choosing. You hope they'll meet your standards. You may even find you want to take them with you as insurance against future cosmetic distress.

Designing for a captive audience is almost the exact opposite of designing for shelf-competitive graphics. It's much closer to a franchise or vertical retail situation, where you have total control over the environment in which the product resides. Understanding the competition has some bearing on your strategy, but there is no competition sitting on the shelf next to your product. You must focus on the intricate details of the amenities and services offered, the details that truly capture your client's brand identity.

In the mid-1980s, Hyatt Hotels asked us to create a line of amenities for its worldwide hotel chain. Each year Hyatt places approximately 12 million one-ounce bottles of shampoo and hair conditioner in over 50,000 bathrooms around the globe. Hyatt officials knew that these generically packaged amenities did not express the sense of style the hotel chain was cultivating. Hyatt's straightforward brief required that we design a line of attractive containers that captured Hyatt's image, complemented

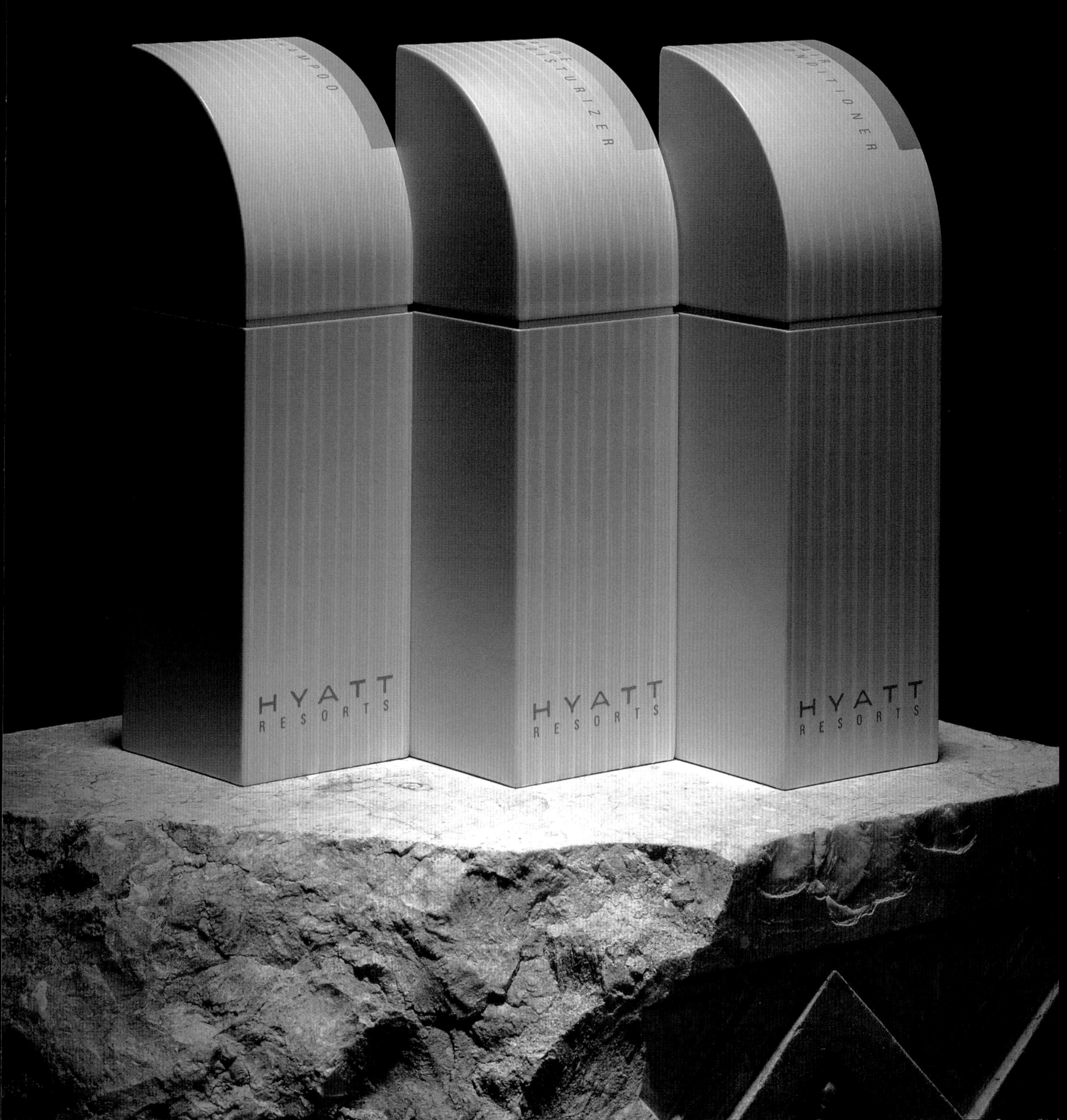
HYATT
RESORTS
HYATT
RESORTS
HYATT
RESORTS

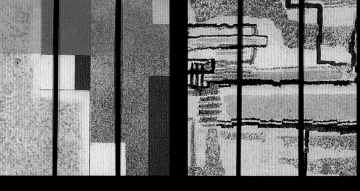

We started out with an ambitious direction for the Hyatt project. Numerous patterns were created so that individual hotels could personalize the surface of their amenities' packages. When we examined the production implications of such an undertaking, however, we opted for a more practical, simple, and uniform solution.

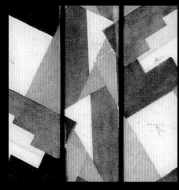
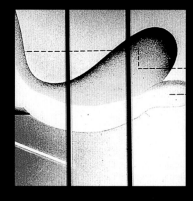

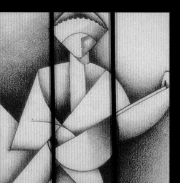
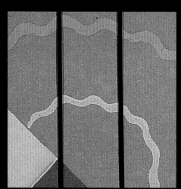

its bathroom environments, and also encouraged guests to take them along as reusable gift boxes for home, office, or bathroom display. Our aesthetic positioning was upper mainstream, appealing to a wide range of tastes and customers. As our research progressed, we gravitated toward minimal, geometric shapes that suggested the lines and curves of sculpture; we then combined these shapes with a subtle color palette and typography. The Hyatt brand name is a refined presence at the bottom of the package.

Looking back on this design, it's interesting to note how continually and quickly our consciousness of shapes evolves. Our design was an excellent solution for the 1980s, but today, to current sensibilities, the comps and models we discarded as too cutting edge seem much more appropriate.

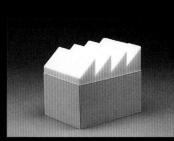

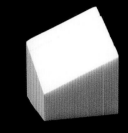

Exploration of Shapes and Structures

While developing an aesthetic form for shampoo and lotion containers to reflect the visual identity of Hyatt Hotels, we explored numerous geometric shapes. Our designs suggested the lines and curves of architecture or sculpture, but also provided solutions that would easily fit into the home.

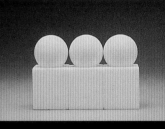

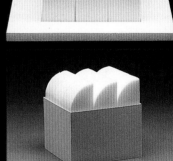

Perhaps in the future this type of complimentary amenity will give way altogether to more functional and environmentally efficient dispenser systems. Waste reduction and biodegradability are real concerns that will present different design problems in the future. The messages customers take home then might not be in the form of a complimentary product, but in the lingering memory of an excellent, intelligent, harmonious experience.

The amenity packaging for the shampoo, hair conditioner, and mending kit that you find in your hotel room is a good example of how to make a lasting impression with a whisper rather than a shout.

ENVIRONMENTAL GRAPHIC DESIGN

Packaging Buildings and Other Feats
of Environmental Graphics

Environmental graphics can be defined as signage, architectural color, banners, furniture, signature lighting, exhibit design, and in some instances, interior and exterior architecture. These elements "package" a building. Just as packages must achieve a sense of integrity with the products they contain, environmental graphics must remain true to their surroundings. When successful, they do much more than communicate functional information: they stir emotions such as nostalgia, excitement, or curiosity; they inform, direct, and educate us through visual imagery, color, typography, and form.

To create imagery that enhances rather than detracts from the environment, designers must work closely with all related disciplines – architecture, interior architecture, and environmental graphics – with attention to colors, materials, and the ways in which the space will be used. The ultimate goal is a seamless presentation – as though the design were orchestrated by one person with a single vision. "Programming" is the backbone of the field: an intimate understanding of the larger context of the building so that specific design solutions also relate to the broader whole. By identifying with the spirit behind the architectural design, environmental graphics can communicate on sensory and emotional levels.

Fulfilling the marketing demands of a specific project includes attracting people to the space, keeping them excited and stimulated once there, and making sure they don't get lost. To satisfy ourselves, however, we continually strive to find unique solutions for each project and make contributions to the field, achieving graphics that are fresh and unpredictable, that challenge the boundaries of this dynamic field, and that bridge the tension between the timeless and the unconventional.

Instill a Sense of History and Create Functional Signage
Through Environmental Graphics

The Hills Brothers Plaza Building is one of the last remaining brick industrial structures that epitomized the San Francisco waterfront in years gone by. At the time of its construction in 1926, the facility was considered state of the art. For over 60 years, it functioned as the main processing plant and corporate headquarters for Hills Brothers Coffee, Inc. In 1991, the landmark building was preserved and renovated as an integral part of the Hills Plaza development. Hills Plaza is a multi-use complex including office, retail, and residential space. It was designed to complement the existing structure's Romanesque architectural style. Two main buildings are gracefully joined by a large bay-view courtyard plaza.

The environmental graphics required a distinctive approach to satisfy the functional objectives as well as capture the historic ambience of this special site. We wanted the signage to reflect the romance of an older time, to recreate some of the nostalgia of the '20s and '30s, when the original building was constructed, and also to achieve an appropriate contemporary enhancement of the architectural statement.

62

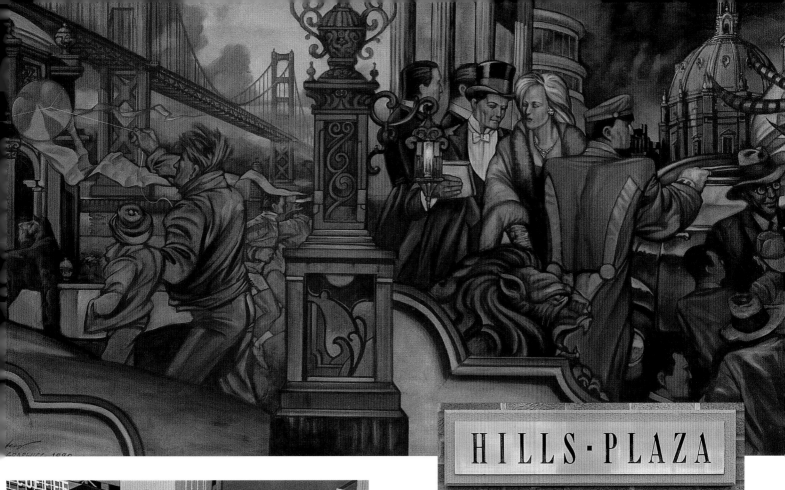

Waterfront Development

A historic building sandwiched between modern structures on the Embarcadero, Hills Brothers Plaza looks out onto the San Francisco Bay and the bridge connecting Berkeley and Oakland with San Francisco. At right, a model storefront shows the design approach for the signage.

Mural Motif

The concept driving the environmental graphics involved the creation of three different murals in the WPA style, depicting scenes from various periods of San Francisco's history. These would be applied to signage as a way of enhancing the sense of history of this classic building.

Drawing Attention to the Architecture

Deliveries were originally made to this part of the building, which has now become integrated into the courtyard connecting the two wings of the complex. Below are proposed banner placements, intended to focus attention on this outstanding architectural element.

Courtyard Banners

Permanent banners add color to the courtyard. Made from metal to withstand the weather, they feature accents of turquoise, patina, purple, blue, and yellow.

Historical License

In creating a historical overview of San Francisco we exercised liberal license, selecting people and events that shaped the city: the Golden Gate and Bay bridges, Chinatown, the World's Fair, the modern Financial District. The 1906 earthquake was intentionally omitted. At right, the signage benefits directly from the mural's rich imagery.

Stairs

Directional Flow

The mandatory directional signage took advantage of the typography and color scheme chosen for the rest of the project.

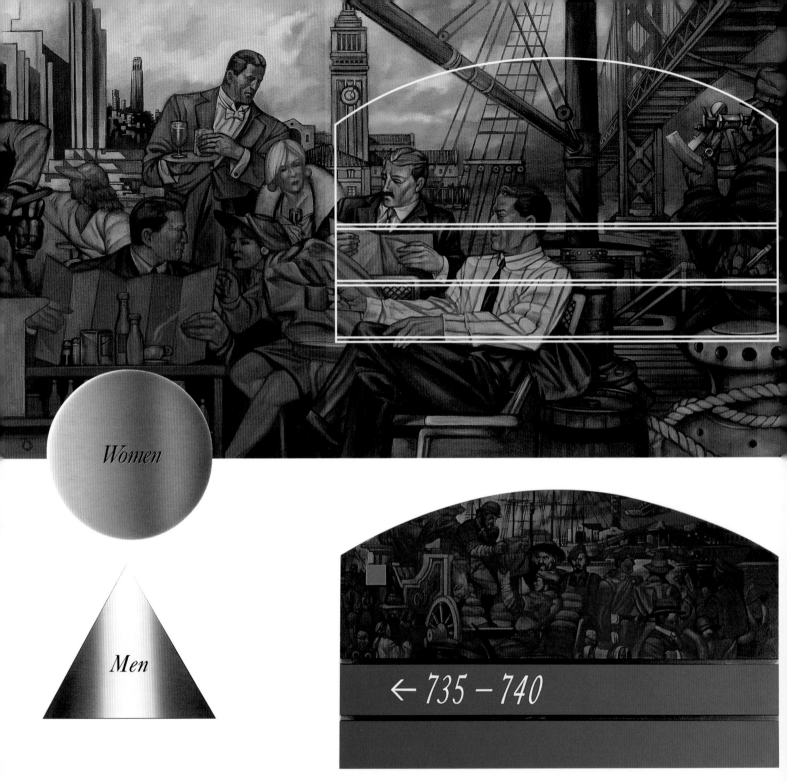

Women

Men

← 735 – 740

No Detail Is Small   *The signs demarcating each floor, building suite, and parking entrance borrowed a different scene from the mural. Although signs for restrooms must adhere to strict codes, we chose to give women and men distinct geometric shapes.*

PARKING

Our idea was to develop one massive mural that would show various aspects of the city's development. We could then derive scenes and elements from the painting, using them for identity and directional signage throughout the pedestrian flow. The mural was done in oils by David McMacken and patterned after the WPA paintings of that era. We also relied on architectural features to direct the visual vocabulary of the environmental graphics. The arch, a motif recurring throughout the complex, influenced the shapes of the signage. The color teal, an accent tone appearing on the aluminum window frames, was used as a principal color. Like the architecture itself, the typography we chose combined past and present – a classical typeface with a modern sensibility.

The Permanence of Change

The San Francisco Fashion Center – situated in a picturesque, renovated warehouse in the South of Market district – is an invaluable resource for Northern California's burgeoning fashion industry. John Portman & Associates of Atlanta, Georgia, served as the architectural designers for this enormous undertaking. We were brought into the project in the early stages to ensure that the signage and environmental graphics complemented and enhanced the architectural and emotional aspects of the building.

The dynamics of change set the tone and direction for the environmental graphics. Change is not only at the core of the fashion industry, it's also the very essence of an exhibition center. With over 100,000 square feet of continually evolving booth space and 550 permanent showrooms and services, a major priority for the project was versatility. One requirement was a signage system that could be tailored to accommodate almost any imaginable situation, from international fashion fairs and trade shows to social events. Throughout the Center, the graphics had to be sophisticated and energetic enough to appeal to the wide range of people who would be visiting or working in the building.

LEVEL

6

3202 _TO_ **3202**
3121 _TO_ **3126**
3262 _TO_ **3280**

3129 _TO_ **3345**
3121 _TO_ **3129**
3262 _TO_ **3284**

3
FLOOR LEVEL

Three-Dimensional Signage

The materials and graphic elements of the directory signage above were intentionally layered to create depth and color. In addition to focusing visitors' attention on the building's identity, the signage lends a sculptural quality to the space. Our design team enhanced the Fashion Center logo, which appears on signs and banners inside and outside the building.

Architecture, interior architecture, and environmental graphics must be an integrated family.

Color Scheming

Our goal was to develop a color scheme that would not compete with the architecture or any exhibit that might be taking place in the Center. Since the materials used in the building construction featured soft and muted tones, we felt the signage could reflect some of the excitement and color of the fashion industry. At right, banners made from synthetic fabric provide a fresh complement to the brick exterior. Inside, environmental graphics combine playfulness and functionality.

Flexible and Directional

The solution for the directional signage was to create a layered, sculptural element with the main focus on flexibility. The small black signs can easily be replaced and tailored to the specific requirements of any event.

Thoroughfares

The Fashion Center is a popular venue for fashion and trade fairs, attracting thousands of visitors each day. Where there is heavy foot traffic, directional signs are larger but still can be changed to accommodate each event and allow visitors to navigate the area with ease.

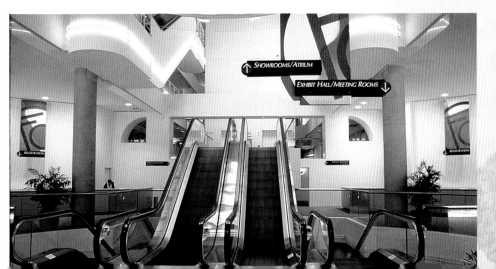

Because the interior and exterior architecture employed a neutral color scheme, we saw an opportunity to inject vitality through signage. By combining a vibrant color palette with abstract graphic shapes and forms, we created a sense of exuberance evocative of the fast pace of the fashion business. Another primary design focus was the interchangeable signage system: from directional signs to directories, all informational panels can be replaced or updated using sliding or magnetic-backed components.

These solutions are best achieved by placing the project in its proper context. In the case of the San Francisco Fashion Center, by understanding the nature of the space we were able to create dynamic environmental graphics and signage as colorful and variable as the apparel industry itself.

POSTERS

Posters occasionally offer the opportunity to violate my philosophy of not imposing a personal style on a design assignment.

Designing posters for lithography and screen-printing is currently my favorite form of personal expression. It's a whisper from my printmaking past, a medium that seems to have been eclipsed for the most part by electronic communication. Posters offer the opportunity to violate my philosophy of refraining from imposing a personal style on an assignment. My excuse is that most of these assignments are *pro bono* and usually concern subjects about which I have an opinion: I can be subjective in these cases because the subject and I have a common viewpoint.

Posters also provide me the opportunity to work alone – without the entire design team, whom I indeed enjoy – and I inevitably find the exercise a healthy diversion. But then there are those desperate occasions when the entire studio, in great sympathy for my fast-approaching deadline and overambitious promise, pitches in to help.

On occasion, with these noncritical-deadline projects, I find myself immersed in too much visual play – concocting too many design alternatives and running the danger of departing from what a fast-reading poster requires as opposed to the personal statement of a fine art print. The danger is a loss of spontaneity, and unwarranted compromises. Rather than emphasizing the message to be communicated, the project evolves into an aesthetic expression without objectivity. The line between being a poster and being a commemorative limited-edition print becomes fuzzy; what usually follows is a visual that is neither a print nor a poster, but decoration. I've been there a few times. Optimally, a poster should provide a degree of visual pleasure that will keep it hanging on the wall long after its primary verbal message has been communicated.

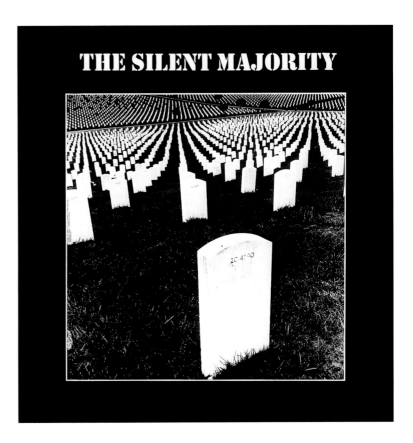

"Hair"

It was the 1960s, and the Broadway musical "Hair" was shocking the sensibilities of conservative Americans from coast to coast. This poster, featuring a photograph by Lars Speyer, was commissioned for the San Francisco opening of the show. The lyrics of "Aquarius" adorn and frame the image, which was also a statement of the hip '60s. Late afternoon light and the dye-transfer process killed much of the funky background detail and gave all the forms a rich, dark texture.

A Personal Statement

Inspired by then-President Richard Nixon's phrase "silent majority," this poster became a popular expression of the Vietnam situation in 1969 and is now in numerous collections. When I heard the comment "silent majority and silent Americans," the first thing that came to mind was a graveyard; "silent majority" sounded unique, and more interesting when used by itself. A fast call to photographer Lars Speyer got me a black-and-white image of a military graveyard. My black border and simple stenciled typeface confirmed the statement. The poster was designed in one day, printed and on the street in three days.

Boudin

The Boudin poster is part of a graphic-design program developed for the original French bread bakery in San Francisco. The primary design objective was to establish the product as the region's finest. This poster succeeds by reinforcing the brand's European heritage while communicating the bread's fresh, homemade quality through a crisp, rich use of typography and primary colors on a white background. A special limited-edition eight-color lithograph was published for special collections.

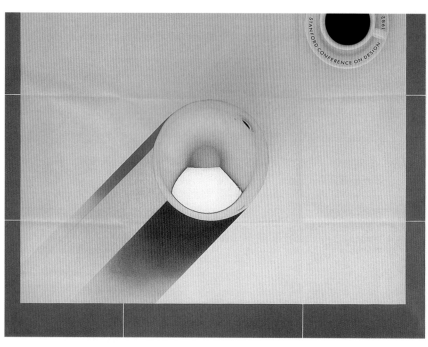

1982 Stanford Design Conference

This poster utilized two strong symbols: a cup of coffee reflecting the intimacy of the conference, and a chrome globe that served as a 360° visual reflector shown as if moving in space and sitting on a tablecloth. It looks as though it's on a collision path with the cup of coffee, but it's not. Perhaps it is a bit abstract; it is not my usual approach to a poster.

San Francisco International Airport

When the San Francisco International Airport unveiled its new modern facilities in 1983, the city felt it was a good time to promote the airport's status as a major gateway to international destinations. The facility's curvilinear architecture is portrayed in the central portion of the poster. The symbols of clouds, airliner, and world, the blue-green color, and the decorative typographic placement say the rest. The posters were mailed to business and civic leaders nationwide and were sold in airport gift stores. We also designed a press kit and other collateral material as part of the airport's identity package.

Festa Italiana

Festa Italiana, an extremely popular festival held every October in San Francisco, is a four-day event that attracts thousands of Italian Americans (and hundreds who just wish they were). The poster for the first Festa, held in 1983, sports Italy's national colors and highlights the main attractions of the event: dance, drink, food, fun, and Italian culture.

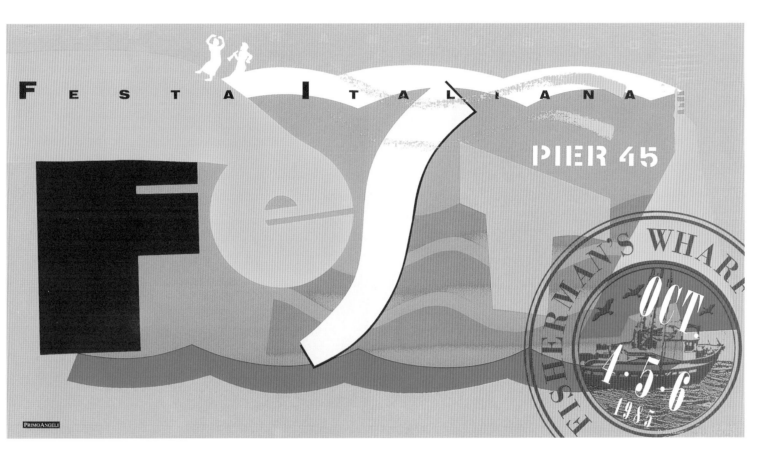

Festa Italiana 85

By 1985, Festa Italiana was attracting a broad cross-section of the Bay Area's population, so I switched to a more contemporary style to boost the event's widening appeal, especially among youthful attendees. Some of the older North Beach Italians didn't care for it; it was my last Festa poster.

Molinari

This promotional poster marks the 93rd anniversary of P. G. Molinari & Sons delicatessen. Why the 93rd? It sounded like a good idea at the time. I jammed this composition with typography, Italian imagery, cancellation marks, signatures, USDA meat stamps, an illustration of Coit Tower, and a portrait of founder P. G. Molinari – all in eight colors and a glossy finish. Boy, that's Italian!

The Theme Was Connections

My own was a dessert connection for this Simpson Paper company poster series. The dessert goblet and the two figures alternate in positive and negative form. The copy is from e. e. cummings, and reads: "While you and I have lips and voices which are for kissing and to sing with, who cares if some one-eyed son-of-a-bitch invents an instrument to measure spring with."

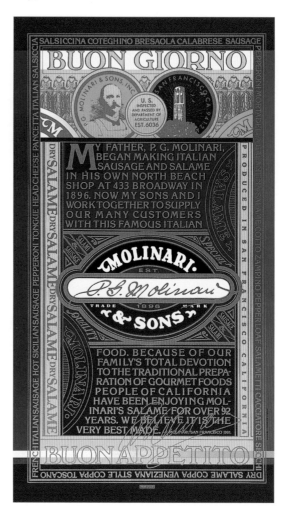

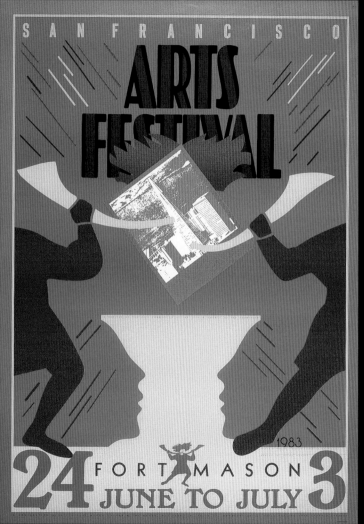

San Francisco
Fine Arts Festival

Every year the San Francisco
Fine Arts Festival brings
together artisans, craftspeople,
and others from the city's art
community to exhibit their
work. This poster was
commissioned in 1983 by the
Arts Commission of the City
and County of San Francisco.
The symbols represented here
have to provide for the
performing as well as applied
arts: horns, figures in
movement, faces, vases, and
a Polaroid of the city with
flashing flames against
the typographic statement
"Arts Festival."

Illuminating the Bridge

As a pro bono project for the City of San Francisco, we designed the visuals for the celebration of the 50th anniversary of the opening of the Golden Gate Bridge. The friends of the Golden Gate Bridge asked us to design the identity and adapt the logo for use as a poster to commemorate the majestic structure and its new permanent lighting. We created an image that accentuates the bridge's Art Deco features and suggests illumination and celebration. The logo was used as an identity mark in all planning and promotion for the event.

Sydney Visits San Francisco

Sponsored by Qantas, this poster promotes
and commemorates the San Francisco–Sydney
Sister Committee's yearly event. It was printed
on a heavy high-gloss stock by Williams
Lithograph Company of San Francisco.
I utilized the computer and an X-ACTO knife
as a cut-and-paste design technique.

San Francisco Visits Sydney

This poster celebrates San Francisco
week in Sydney and was accomplished
again in cooperation with Williams
Lithograph Company of San Francisco.
It is essentially a celebration of cultural
and commercial interests. I used the
image of the TransAmerica building
topped with an olive as a symbol for
party merrymaking (it had always been
my secret desire to skewer a giant olive
on the tip of the TransAmerica pyramid).

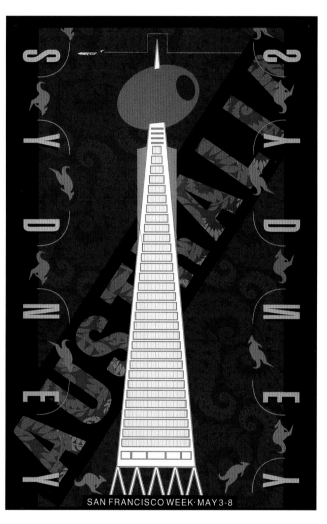

More Sister Cities

In February 1988, the city of Hong Kong invited San Francisco business leaders, Mayor Dianne Feinstein and other city officials, and the San Francisco Symphony to a week-long celebration of the long-standing cultural and commercial relationship between Hong Kong and San Francisco. As a member of the delegation, I created this poster, loaded with symbols from both cities, to commemorate the event.

Protesting the Protest and the Politically Correct

Occasionally there are pro bono projects that require nerves of steel to complete. San Francisco was supposed to stage the country's biggest celebration of the 500th Anniversary of Columbus's Discovery of America but, for reasons still unclear, the plans collapsed. Here is the story: I was asked by the quincentenary committee to do the official commemorative poster. Pro bono, of course. After several

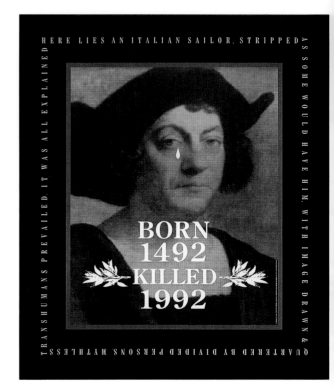

weeks and several designs and several thousands of dollars in labor time, here's what I ran into: "Don't show any of the caravels — they marked the end of Indian civilization. No Indians. No Maltese cross. No world or globe — too Old World Eurocentric. No Spanish, Italian, or U.S. colors. No sailors, no Columbus, no heroes." The politically correct committee finally decided not to print anything so as not to offend anyone except the designer. This poster was my personal statement of the situation, silk-screened in black and white. The copy framing the image reads: "Here lies an Italian sailor, stripped as some would have him, with image drawn and quartered by divided persons. Mythless transhumans prevailed. It was all explained."

California Mission Blankets

Pendleton Woolen Mills commissioned me to design a collector-quality, signed, limited-edition series of blankets featuring the 21 missions of California. The first blanket in the series celebrates Mission Dolores, completed in 1791 at 16th and Dolores Streets in San Francisco, the sixth mission undertaken by Father Junipero Serra. Following the design for the blanket, the limited-run poster for the Mission Dolores blanket is silk-screened in six colors on an uncoated paper stock. Both blanket and poster were executed through hand-drawn imagery and photographic scans and then refined on the Macintosh computer with Adobe software. The blanket and poster were sold in Pendleton locations throughout California.

Grace Cathedral

This poster commemorates the silver anniversary of one of San Francisco's most prominent cathedrals, Grace Cathedral, and was used as a fund-raiser for an extensive rehabilitation program commissioned by the Very Reverend Dean Alan Jones. Loaded with religious symbolism, it's a giant four-color lithographic print on an enamel stock.

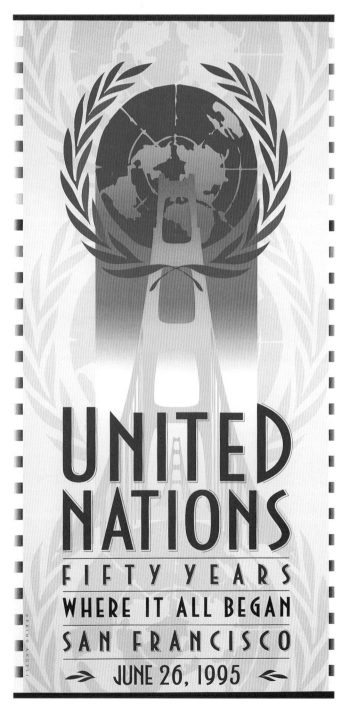

UN50

Promoting the worldwide celebration of the 50th anniversary of San Francisco as the site of the signing of the United Nations Charter, this poster features a natural combination of symbols in the intermingling of the Golden Gate Bridge with the United Nations trademark. The poster graphics portray the essential look we utilized in the overall visuals for this event. San Francisco superwoman Charlotte Mailliard Swig brought this celebration to fruition.

An Unorthodox Approach to Product Development

With market research confirming the same grim statistics year after year – that 80 percent of the 20,000 new products introduced annually in the United States ultimately fail – we thought the times demanded a new approach to product development. In the marketplace, the package is perceived as the actual product; why not take advantage of this fact? Why not develop finished-looking packages with highly competitive brands and product names first, before creating the products? Critique and qualify them internally without consumers' opinions, gather together those judged most likely to succeed, and turn them over to consumer testing. The highest-rated packages/products then can be sent to Research & Development for product manufacturing.

At first our critics called it ridiculous. We called it RapidAccess®. And that's what it is: a fast way in. In the case of "frequent repeat purchase," shelf-competitive items for which the package fulfills an essential function, RapidAccess® offers an unconventional approach to new product development. Acting as a creative catalyst, it forces companies to "think out of the box" of traditional product design by conceptualizing the package first, not the product. This creative orientation frequently introduces clients to a wide range of unexpected product categories beyond the all-important but sometimes limited world of line extensions.

Rough sketches, flat artwork, and typed briefs fail to stir the imagination with the same intensity as a perceived, real product. With RapidAccess®, new ideas are quickly transformed into three-dimensional comps in Full Market Dress™. (These complete product representations, called "comps" by marketers and designers, include brand names and identities, alternative packaging graphics, optional package structures, and selling copy. The graphics, materials, and weight of a comp are as close as possible to those of an actual finished product.)

In another break with convention, RapidAccess® keeps consumer focus groups out of the design process until creative teams have fully realized their ideas, thus challenging the popular notion that "the customer is always right" and should therefore dictate the design process. The logic is simple: "Tell us what you want, we'll make it, and you'll buy it." But we feel it's time to give the freedom and responsibility back to design teams, who are often too sub-

RapidAccess®:

* *Design the ideal package before the product.*
* *Ignore the consumer until the creative process is complete.*
* *Create the most realistic prototypes possible.*
* *Market test and rate the prototypes.*
* *Produce the item to fit the prototype package of the consumer's choice.*

In the marketplace, the package is perceived as the actual product; why not take advantage of this fact? Why not develop finished-looking packages with highly competitive brands and product names first, before creating the products?

servient – every step of the way – to over-analysis through consumer testing. RapidAccess® allows the creative team's best ideas to surface, and can also be instrumental in eliciting more accurate results from test groups.

Consumers can be resistant to change. If their feedback unnecessarily inhibits the research stage, it will severely limit development possibilities. Truly, most consumers have neither the vision nor the experience with the creative process to appreciate or critique a work in progress as it relates to the work's ultimate goal. Too often, single components, such as a bottle structure for a beverage, are tested in model shapes. Consumer opinions on a naked bottle out of all graphic context will be misleading and inhibit the product's design and marketability. (See, for example, our experience selecting the bottle for Henry Weinhard's Root Beer, described in the chapter "Shelf-Competitive Products.") Research convincingly demonstrates that consumers presented with mere sketches, models, or descriptions of new products in a controlled environment often give positive feedback. If these same consumer testers had to pay for the same product, however, they might not select it off the market shelf. It's a trap into which marketers have fallen time and again. On the other hand, the preparation and presentation of a super-real-looking prototype – full-color, three-dimensional; visually, verbally, and spiritually complete – has considerable psychological advantages: the prototype is no longer perceived as a "package" but as a "product," and marketers receive a valid critique of the item as a finished whole. The "transference" in this case makes the information more reliable.

Thomas Hine's outstanding 1995 book, *The Total Package*, devoted a chapter to Louis Cheskin's theory of "sensation transference."

Working from the 1930s through the 1960s, Cheskin was a marketing psychologist who conducted pioneering experiments to analyze consumer responses to packages. He found that the consumer ultimately "transfers" the sensations he or she intuits from a package to the end product: in the consumer's mind, there is no difference between package and product. Study after study showed that the same product, packaged in two different ways, will elicit two distinct reactions from respondents. Based on the design of the package, consumers form their expectations of performance, taste, texture, smell, and other qualities. Hine describes RapidAccess® as "the ultimate in sensation transference. First you engineer the sensation, and then you engineer the substance to which the sensation is to be transferred." We might say it another way: not only is the package perceived as the product – in some cases, it may be more important than the product.

In this age of increasingly competitive global markets, RapidAccess® offers the opportunity to explore product possibilities before heavy investments in consumer research, research and development, and product sampling and testing are made. The earlier a company discovers the real potential of a product to attract consumers, the sooner it becomes a competitive item. RapidAccess® doesn't supplant orthodox research and development but augments it. The goal remains to create outstanding products that consumers want to purchase on a repeat basis. From what I have heard in conversations and working sessions, Research & Development people agree that it is easier to formulate a product from a pretested, finished, realistic package than from a bare written brief.

Is RapidAccess® an ego-driven heresy through which we graphic artists hope to fan the flames of consumption and force open design opportunities? Not at all. Designing "out of the box" is quite simply a method for developing clear visual targets and providing inspiration for Research & Development, the product creator. It aims to reverse the failure rate of new products, abolish the waste of ineffectiveness, and uncover possibilities for successful, on-target new products. And judging from our growing list of clients, we have tapped into an enormously valuable resource. For more detailed information on the RapidAccess® methodology, refer to my article in the May–June 1995 issue of *Business Horizons* magazine.

Designing Out of the Box

Several years ago we designed the corporate brand identity and packaging for Just Desserts, a company well known in California for producing premium, fresh-baked goods distributed through its chain of retail-bakery coffee houses. More recently, Just Desserts decided it was time to expand its distribution, then limited to outlets within a 12- to 24-hour radius of its production facilities for reasons of freshness, by developing a line of shelf-stable products. In response, I proposed to search for a faster, less expensive method for new-product development, and took the first step in formulating the radical concept that eventually became RapidAccess®. Starting with a broad concept – dessert products with extended shelf-life as opposed to goods baked fresh daily – RapidAccess® provided a springboard for ideas. Working closely with the Just Desserts team, we generated a wide range of product options. Each member of our design team pursued a single

The Power of Suggestion

In brainstorming for a variety of potential shelf-stable products, we came up with short bread, biscotti, and Irish tea-pot cookies – all stemming directly from Just Desserts' line of cakes, pies, and other delectables. Other candidates included chocolate fudge sauce and crunchy toppings for ice cream sundaes. Borrowing from the company's established imagery, the realistic three-dimensional comps for these packages created the illusion of an already existing extended family of products.

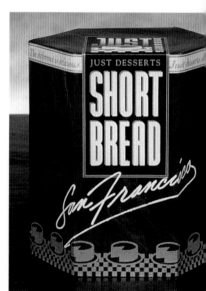

94

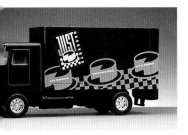

Marketing Opportunity

Advertising and printed materials, packaging, and environmental graphics aren't the only applications for building brand awareness. The broad-scale sides of delivery vehicles present an excellent opportunity to show a company on the move.

Sweet Foundation

Some years ago, we designed the identity for Just Desserts, known throughout the Bay Area for baked goods sold at retail and in fine restaurants.

aspect of a prospective product: packaging, product names, and tag lines.

Once these packaging concepts were considered and critiqued by marketing and production executives, the packages, brands, and products were mixed and remixed. In one instance, a concept initially conceived for a box was switched to a printed octagonal package; in another, a concept proposed for a can was matched to a jar. This exploratory work offered an unprecedented opportunity to consider new product ideas. Being able to pick up and hold actual three-dimensional product packages stimulated a free flow of ideas within the team.

The finalists included ice-cream toppings, Italian biscotti, Irish tea-pot cookies, and other potential products illustrated in this chapter. Based on its marketing instincts and experience, Just Desserts selected the biscotti as its new product candidate and chose an attention-grabbing tapered carton for the package.

Generate new concepts for a company interested in expanding from retail distribution to shelf-competitive wholesale markets.

Italian Sensibilities

For the Just Desserts biscotti project, we illustrated aroma, texture, and a sense of classic Italy to deliver the look of an upper mainstream Italian product.

Authentic Accidents

It was renowned Italian photographer/designer Roberto Carra who told us that, even though the graphics were illustrated, we had precisely captured the style of traditional biscotti packages from Tuscany. The swirl pattern on the box, typical of fine Florentine handmade paper, suggests the creamy mixture of the ingredients. The tile border was another in a remarkable collection of authentic elements.

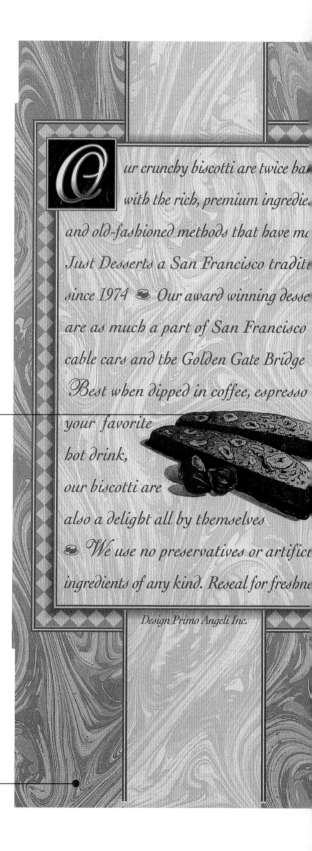

Design Primo Angeli Inc.

96

San Francisco

JUST DESSERTS

Biscotti

Hazelnuts, Sugar, Unbleach-
ed Enriched Flour (wheat
flour, malted barley flour,
niacin, iron, thiamin mono-
nitrate, riboflavin), Semi-
sweet Chocolate, Fresh Whole
Eggs, Grade AA Butter,
Spice, Natural Process Cocoa, Instant
Coffee, Salt, Baking Powder.

◆◆◆

Just Desserts, 1970 Carroll Avenue
San Francisco California, 94124

ALL NATURAL

CHOCOLATE DIPPED HAZELNUT

NO PRESERVATIVES

NET WT. 8 OZ.

Now that so many in the world around
us are striving to embrace the rewards
of freedom and democracy, we have the
opportunity to address the challenges we
face at home rather than wasting billions
of dollars on a threat that no longer exists.

◆◆◆

Let's re-invest in our country's future... our
children, our schools, our environment and
economic opportunity for all of our citizens.

◆◆◆

Join the Campaign for New Priorities
and help get America invested in our
future again. Call 1-800-92 ACTION.

This new product/package, along with two other highly ranked concepts, were fully developed by the design group and presented to marketing and management, then turned over to R&D, who created the actual shelf-stable biscotti product.

For a medium-sized company such as Just Desserts, introducing a new product can be an enormous venture. RapidAccess® provided a full-dimensional "picture" and description of the product, and thus served as a detailed road map that guided R&D's efforts and expedited its development of the successful final products. Following the biscotti, Just Desserts' ice-cream toppings appeared on grocery shelves in late 1995.

By making the package more important than the product, RapidAccess® is turning tradition on its head. This new process can be quicker, less expensive, more productive, and less wasteful than traditional methods for developing new products.

And to Top Things Off...

Just Desserts' toppings were created for distribution in their retail outlets to accompany their cake line. We designed a look for the packaging that was rich, scrumptious, and both homey and upscale.

Create an immediately recognizable visual symbol
for the United States' first international film festival,
the San Francisco International Film Festival

Packaging the 38th Annual San Francisco International Film Festival – a celebration of the 100th anniversary of film – was exceptionally exciting because it presented us with a diverse range of design vehicles. John Diefenbach, a director of the San Francisco Film Society, approached us with clear objectives for positioning the imagery of the event. Peter Scarlet, president, and publications officer Miguel Pendás requested a trademark that would visually distinguish the 1995 festival, serve as the brand identity for future festivals, and double as a corporate identity for the San Francisco Film Society.

By my standards, a great trademark is appropriate, dynamic, distinctive, memorable, and unique. A great trademark also serves as a face and as a thumbprint for a corporation, and must be flexible enough to be printed in various sizes, colors, and formats. The operating principle here is the subtle but important difference between being distinctive and being unique: diverse visual identities can share distinctiveness of manner or style – but not uniqueness. Satisfying both of these demands is key in capturing those ever-elusive qualities: originality and memorability.

SAN FRANCISCO
INTERNATIONAL
FILM FESTIVAL

The United States' oldest international film festival has always
attracted a notable gathering of talent; this year, as in past years,
the spotlight would be on directors rather than stars, and the
new trademark must reflect this focus. Since this was an
international festival, we settled on a pictogram –
a universal, nonverbal symbol – portraying the director in
motion at the center of the film-making process,

Power of the Pictogram

The pictogram presented an effective way to communicate the message of the festival to an international audience.

a camera in one hand and a megaphone in the other. Because it was the debut for this new image direction, the trademark would occupy a prominent position on posters, banners, and a host of other materials, from containers and T-shirts to the Society's corporate letterhead.

An outstanding client is essential to producing excellent work. The openness fostered by the San Francisco Film Society was just what was necessary to create a dynamic working partnership. The client brought all the right ingredients to the table: a clear concept and objectives for positioning, a willingness to allow the best features of the work to surface, and, most important, sufficient time in which to explore a number of design possibilities. The new San Francisco International Film Festival identity places the film directors, the event organizers, and the festival itself in the proper limelight.

Point of Sale

The bold graphic logo offered festival organizers an excellent opportunity to produce event-related caps, mugs, and T-shirts.

Meeting of the Media

The festival poster was created through a unique hybrid of media. The first phase of the artwork was completed using Adobe Illustrator. We then took a CalComp color printout of the poster background and blended the colors with WD-40, an aerosol lubricant, to achieve a rich, textured effect. Next, this collage was photographed and rescanned into the layout before the San Francisco Film Society trademark was superimposed on a diagonal. This technique achieved a painterly result by combining industrial-age WD-40 with information-age computer technology.

The challenge: 500 design firms vying for an opportunity to create the visual landscape for the 1996 Olympic Games in Atlanta. Should we even bother to apply? We've taken on some huge, complex projects in our past, but this one would place us center stage with the entire world looking on.

The selection process was not for the weak of heart. It involved six months of screening, multiple checkpoints, and intense paperwork. The committee narrowed the candidates from 500 to 30 to 10, and finally we were called to Atlanta to make a capabilities presentation. In late 1993, the Atlanta Committee for the Olympic

The Look

The "Look of the Games" consisted of a family of identifying elements: the quilt of leaves, the Landor torch (shown above), and the pictograms.

Games (ACOG) selected five design firms – spread across the country – to create, together, the graphics for the 26th Olympiad.

The newly designated Olympics design team included Copeland Hirthler/Murrell, Atlanta (represented by Brad Copeland); Jones Worley Design, Atlanta (represented by Barry Worley); Boston-based Favermann Design (represented by Mark Favermann); Malcolm Grear Designers Inc., Providence, Rhode Island (represented by Malcolm Grear); and our firm in San Francisco. This diverse team was coordinated by Oscar Harris, from the Atlanta-based architectural firm of Turner Associates. Ginger Watkins, ACOG's managing director of corporate services, was in charge of selecting the design team and also managed our design direction.

So now we had five independent design groups with distinct talents, work styles, reputations, and specializations. None of us had ever met, let alone worked together. How could a group of strangers – artists with their own working methods and strong egos – create a harmonious, engaging look for this monumental event? I kept reminding myself that my own studio is made up of designers from many different cultures, but our common purpose always has been to focus on what is unique about a project; to let the assign-

ment dictate the tone and style. I hoped that my teammates' approach would be the same.

In early 1994, we traveled to Atlanta for the first of many working sessions. We began that first meeting with introductions and comments from William Porter Payne, president and CEO of ACOG. "This is the biggest Olympic Games, and it will be the most spectacular – a once-in-a-lifetime experience that will never come again," he told us. "I want you to knock the socks off the world for this one."

Then we were introduced to the issues that would guide our work. ACOG supplied five distinct personality statements for visual translation:

Atlanta, the South, the Olympic Games, 100 years of modern competition, and more abstractly, the human attributes of harmony, grace, and radiance. Each firm was to work on one premise.

Our design team's first interactive effort was to distill the five messages into a more manageable three, with all working on one target instead of each focusing on a separate positioning statement. We ended up with the centennial of the Games, the South, and the human spirit. They are all so closely related that, in effect, they made one major personality statement.

By the end of the first meeting, we knew we had to solidify the spirit of our collaboration.

Two symbols emerged for a flexible yet distinctive "Look of the Games": the communal art form of quilting and the South's lush landscape.

No matter what any of us did individually, we would be critiqued as one entity. The five firms formed one team, so we gave it a working title: "Design Five."

The team's agreed-on working approach helped bring harmony and unity to the project. Although we returned to our respective studios to work on roughs (developing the basic look and key elements such as the torch, banners, signage, uniforms, and structural graphics), we all had to operate using 20"x30" boards. No one would have a "bells and whistles" advantage over anyone else; the ideas would have to shine through.

After some reflection, and inspired in part by the mandated 20"x30" boards, my studio took an approach slightly contrary to the original charter. Rather than solve individual items, we focused on a general feel for the Olympics, using the three positioning statements; that is, we visually interpreted the various aspects of the positioning statements on individual boards, then

The Quilt

Our quilt design served as the umbrella unifying all the fine work of our design collaborators.

Anything could have gone wrong, but our focus was
on what could go right. We didn't go into a lot of detail;
we just kept the composition open and flexible.

mixed and matched the pieces into the three most appropriate compositions. For example, one board showed a runner; another, the facade of one of the facilities; one board depicted the color scheme; another, the signage system. We developed three major wall-mural–sized sets representing the South, the centennial of the modern Olympics, and the Greek origin of the Games, and took these three sets to the first presentation meeting in Atlanta. In the meantime, we kept in touch with the other Design Five members, visiting their studios to see how they were progressing and to get critiques of our efforts.

The second Atlanta meeting, held two months after the first, was a hard working-session to check concepts. Each team put its boards up on a wall in a large conference room. The boards ranged from thumbnails to very slick, tight comps. Then we talked about our work and why we did it the way we did. What followed contributed significantly to both the unity and

The Pictograms

*Used as a nonverbal language worldwide, the pictogram presents a way to circumvent
the Tower of Babel of having many languages at one venue. The 1992 Winter Games
in Lillehammer represented the first time pictograms were relied on as a key identity
element for the Olympics. In Atlanta we used a similar approach for nonverbal
communication as part of the identity of the Games.*

the viability of the design team: we threw all the boards on the floor and started over. Oscar Harris directed us: "Primo, you and Malcolm [Grear] create the main look of the Games from any of the modules, whether they're yours or somebody else's." Then he teamed up the other designers to select a modular grouping of boards to represent signage, color, structure, and "other good ideas." We selected the pieces that would fit. The final selection became a visual assimilation of everyone's work.

In March 1994, all Design Five team members met for an in-depth review and final assignments. ACOG decided who got what, based on our presentations, our general interest, and our areas of specialization. Jones Worley Design was given the signage and typographic standards; Malcolm Grear, the pictograms. Favermann Design and Copeland Hirthler/Murrell would create the banners and fabric fences that surround the different venues. We were assigned the "Look of the Games," the structure graphics, and uniform design.

There was general satisfaction with the design process. The team interaction was extraordinary. Anything could have gone wrong, but our focus was on what could go right for the summer of 1996.

It's Official

Juan Antonio Samaranch, International Olympic Committee President, announced that our poster, of the many that were produced, would be the one to represent the 1996 Olympics. It expresses components of the symbolism derived from our early contributions to the look of the 1996 Olympic Games. In celebration of this centennial anniversary of the modern Olympic Games, the poster's statement is a combination of classic and contemporary values. The design places the athletic figure at the center of the composition and takes on a classic Greek sculptural significance through use of the symbolic star and flame across its torso, defining the human form.

GALLERY

The Absence of a Personal Style

As a child, I used to think that the commercial art world was where artists went after they died in the fine art world, but actually the two are very different visual propositions. One is subjective; the other requires a high degree of objectivity. As a marketing designer, I object to utilizing a set personal style to solve design problems.

We are in this business of communication to help our clients sell their products and services. Essentially, we are given a timeline and a budget to reach an audience for a specific response – a hard reality when someone is counting on you to promote his or her product rather than your portfolio. When that responsibility settles in, you take the path that's best for the product.

This rule entails getting into the shoes of the consumer you are trying to reach, which involves the "Zen" ability to become, not only the archer who is shooting the arrow, but the target as well. Once you achieve that level of enlightenment, you are essentially designing for yourself. In that sense, design becomes personal.

The strength of our design philosophy lies in a diversity of design talents from many different cultures and points of view. We are continually challenging ourselves to focus on what is unique about each product or service. We believe it is essential to allow each assignment to dictate tone and style, and to refine our methods of critically assessing the work in progress.

Del Monte Pasta Sauces

*For Del Monte Pasta Sauces we leveraged the strength of the Del Monte brand name and built a new
canned pasta sauce product around it, making the new entity the hero. This new arrival in the Del Monte
line aimed to attract glass-jar–sauce consumers as well as other canned-sauce consumers into the
Del Monte franchise. Although the typical strategy for pasta sauces is to display the product – either
through product photography on the label in the case of a can, or by making the product visible through
a glass jar – we opted to rely instead on attention to details in typography and illustration to denote
the traditional richness of the product and to build this new product's authentic Italian credentials through
the respected Del Monte name as seen on the high-recognition Del Monte shield trademark.*

Boudin

Designed to wrap bread for the oldest French bread baker in San Francisco, the primary design objective was to establish the product as the region's finest. Boudin bread wrappers feature a short history of sourdough French bread and a recipe drawn from a selection of San Francisco's noted French restaurants. The typography is a source of information and delivers a rich, textural taste appeal. However, had I realized that the wrapper would be printed on high-speed flexography with the poor registration quality that existed at that time, I would not have incorporated the nuances that make up this basic yet ornate configuration. In this instance, ignorance was bliss. The design forced this elemental printing medium to its limit, and it worked.

Cambridge Plan

Making food products visually delectable is one thing, but how do you handle a food substitute? That was the question we faced in designing new packaging for the Cambridge Plan, a line of meal replacements created by well-known dietary researcher Dr. Alan Howard of Cambridge University. Because the product is in fact sweet and flavorful, our answer to the question was luscious photography: a "kitchen art" creation that looks good enough to eat. This non-shelf-competitive product is always sold by sales representatives, therefore front-panel branding is unnecessary. When massed together in a display for presentation, these modular units create a rich, powerful taste appeal.

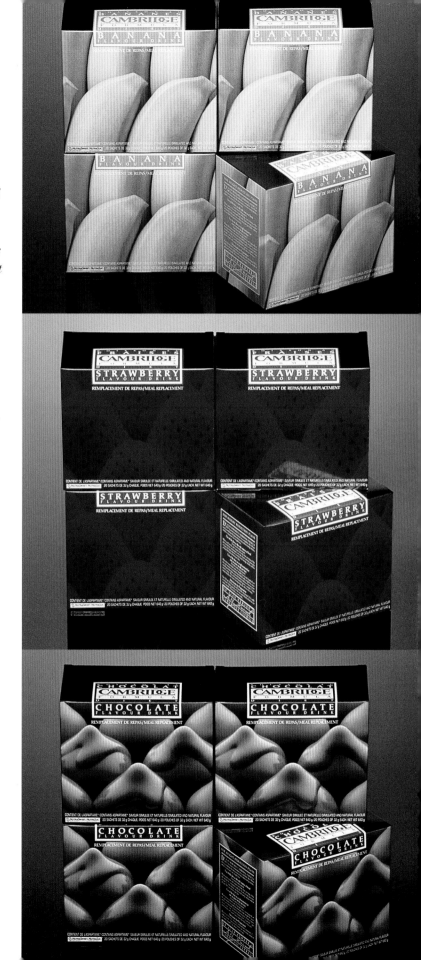

Tutto Mare

This tiny matchbox, representing the brand name of a restaurant from Spectrum Foods, is the tip of the iceberg. It conveys a clear sense of the style that was carried throughout the visual system, which relied on a rich mixture of contemporary and traditional appointments.

Ferris & Roberts

The goal for this assignment was to create packaging for a line of imported English herbal teas with a perceived established English heritage. The project included naming, brand design, packaging design, illustration, finished art, and mechanicals. In naming the project we found a heritage application of existing names within the client firm. The labels were proposed to be run on a mix-and-match single set of colors on one press run. Labels are then hand-applied to a basic black stock-item bag with a see-through window.

116

Torani Syrups

Torani syrups have been popular as flavoring in coffee, soda water, and ice cream since 1925. The R. Torre & Company management and marketing team of Lisa and Paula Lucheta and Melanie Dulbecco provided the positioning statement for this assignment. The objective was to update the line, provide stronger, more legible branding, and reinforce the product's Italian heritage, without disturbing the equity elements on the label.

Nestlé

As Brand Guardian for Nestlé USA, our responsibilities require, not only full attention to all aspects of design, but also a knowledge of the strategic marketing of Nestlé's numerous products worldwide. Shown here are a few of our many design solutions; in the chapter "Shelf-Competitive Products," we address in detail another Nestlé project assignment: Nestlé Butterfinger.

Transporting Guinness Tradition into the Millennium

When Guinness Ireland decided to re-stage its core brand, it assigned us to develop a visual strategy that would increase the brand's relevance for youthful consumers without alienating traditional core-brand consumers. The new branding would be applied to primary and secondary packaging, signage, and—most important, as the majority of Guinness's product is purchased on premise— pub-counter mountings. By retaining proprietary values, updating iconography, and adding color, the new branding system aims at embracing both the progressive and the classic for a powerful statement of credibility, taste appeal, and longevity.

Brian Reid, Guinness Brand Manager, commented, "Guinness first employed Primo Angeli to redesign the packaging for its Harp Lager brand in 1994. This program was a key factor in a brand recovery after many years of decline. The successful re-staging of its crown jewel, Guinness Stout, and the Guinness brand relied heavily on the Angeli team quickly achieving an in-depth understanding of the brand and market dynamics within its unique global context.

Miller Sharp's

Commissioned by Susan Burdett, Director of Creative Development at Miller Brewing Company, this high-impact packaging for the company's non-alcoholic beer is designed to appeal to mainstream beer drinking consumers. The design expressed the feel and taste of a beer that capitalizes on the concept of maintaining an edge: it promises the same enjoyment offered by full-strength beer while promoting the idea of staying "sharp."

Ultra Lucca

An ethnic name is a powerful plus when you are selling homemade pasta in delicatessens and supermarkets. Paul Ferrari of Lucca Delicatessens, Inc., and his partner Larry Cerletti knew we could give Lucca products an edge by creating a distinctive identity. Adding the word "Ultra" helped differentiate these products from the products of other food companies called Lucca.

The explosion of yellow wheat stalks effectively complements the tight, controlled green rectangle, especially against the white background.

The stencil typeface worked for these products in part because it brings an immediacy and freshness to the imagery.

The trademark for Ultra Lucca Delicatessen projects maximum impact, taste appeal, and a fresh contemporary identity throughout all of the company's ethnic retail stores. Ultra Vino is a wine import division of Ultra Lucca.

BeerGear

The BeerGear logo appears on a line of clothing – stitched into caps and shirts and featured on related tags – for BrewMakers, a do-it-yourself beer brewery. Reminiscent of 1930s industrial graphics, the logo makes a bold statement that promotes the idea of work clothes (the work, in this case, being the rewarding task of beer-brewing). The prominent, red BeerGear name, together with the strong yellow background, recalls construction signs associated with serious labor. The crenelated, circular border-imagery doubles as a gear wheel and a bottle cap.

PRIMO ANGELI

Molinari & Sons
Salame Cannister

*When we picked up the
Molinari & Sons assignment in
1981, company president
Peter Giorgi told me, "I'll make
the salame, you make the art."
I don't think he had limited-
edition art in mind, but that's
what we delivered in the form
of a tongue-in-cheek
repackaging announcement.
As a humorous identity
presentation, we produced "the
world's first designer salame."
Seven hundred autographed
and numbered metal cylinders,
each containing a salame, were
sent to select customers and
friends. The package received
accolades from the New York
Package Designers Council
and major art director's clubs.
It also received facetious
worldwide press coverage
as a "designer salame."*

Pete's Brewing
Company

*Pete's Brewing Company,
a microbrewery, wished
to project an identity
closer to that of a super-
premium beer. With the
help of foggy shipyard
images that evoke the
fine ales enjoyed by
serious ale-drinking
"regulars" at a favorite
pub, we upgraded the
company's package
graphics and added two
new flavors: Gold Coast
Lager and Pacific Dry.
Pete's Brewing Company
has grown to be the
fourteenth largest beer
producer in the United
States, and considerably
extended its product
line, since the
introduction of our
original designs.*

AMERICA'S FINEST

PETE'S™

Wicked Ale™

12 Fluid Ounces

OR OPERATE MACHINERY, AND MAY CAUSE HEALTH PROBLEMS

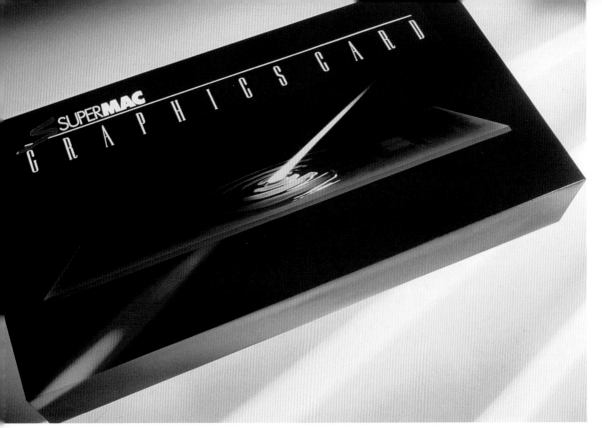

SUPERMAC Graphics Card

The primary objective of this project was to develop a single retail-box design for eight different color-graphics cards. These color cards enhance the color palette and design capability of Macintosh computer systems. We designed an intriguing, high-impact visual for the face of the package, and on the back, a series of labels that incorporate a product description and technical information pertaining to each specific card, making the packaging both practical and cost efficient.

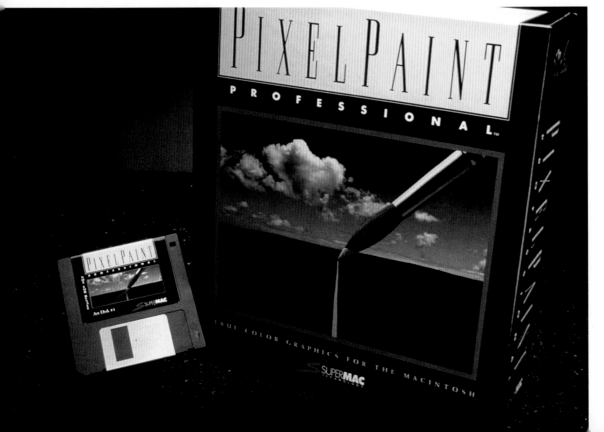

Pixel Paint Professional

Pixel Paint Professional was the first software paint program capable of rendering in 32-bit color. It offered 16.8 million possible colors in contrast to the standard 256. The design problem was to create a package that would convey the sophistication of this, the first product of its kind – a distinctive package that would set it apart from the standard paint programs. The entire package, from concept to mechanical, was designed on the computer, utilizing, appropriately, the product itself.

Quantum

Quantum Corporation, based in Milpitas, California, is a leading supplier of hard disk drives and other information-storage devices worldwide and is recognized as the leading designer and manufacturer of quality data-storage products. In a concerted communications effort to create differentiation among its products over and above product features, the company saw an opportunity to restate its brand mission by defining the brand and consciously developing brand equity. In a full-team effort, representatives from Quantum, PAI, and Quantum's advertising and public relations agencies met to discuss and explore this series of positionings and come up with a visualization of Quantum's new brand promise. The team focused on such elements as type style, imagery, message tone, and effective delivery. Through feedback in these meetings and further refinements, PAI assembled a visual creative brief and proceeded with brand-identity exploration and packaging. Quantum's new look, introduced at the end of 1995, applies to a diverse market that includes Quantum employees, shareholders, financial investors and analysts, the Internet, original equipment manufacturers, the World Wide Web, and retail industries.

Paramount Starlites

*Product entry for the new Paramount retail
operation. One of several applications that also
required naming.*

Shaklee

After the successful introduction of the Shaklee Classic cosmetics and Shaklee Naturals lines,
the company asked us to design a series of fragrances for its Christmas collection. Using stock bottles and
a combination of deco and industrial textures, we delivered this package for Metro, a men's fragrance.

Visa

This Olympic project for Visa USA, designed within Visa's parameters and with restrictions from the Atlanta Committee for the Olympic Games, was beautifully implemented. One of the Committee's requirements was that we use a pictogram from the original family of identities that were developed for the Summer Games. The key contribution to the success of the design was the effective interrelationship with Kate Michels, Creative Director of Marketing Services for Visa USA, who worked to maintain design continuity throughout the program. Our responsibility was to deliver the basic concept and design details that were then successfully implemented by the Visa design team.

Hamm's Building Brochure

The brochure cover shows an application of the 1550 Bryant trademark, designed to highlight the Art Deco elegance of the building that formerly housed Hamm's Brewery and currently houses the offices of Rubin Glickman, Attorney. This towering, 12-story, 177,000-square-foot Bryant Street address, which received a makeover in 1985, is a San Francisco landmark in the heart of the city's industrial and warehouse district. Mr. Glickman and his partner, Susie Tompkins, at the time, of Esprit, purchased the building in 1992 and have made space available for special events and for lease to a variety of tenants.

DC

CAPACITY FOR THE EXTRAORDINARY™

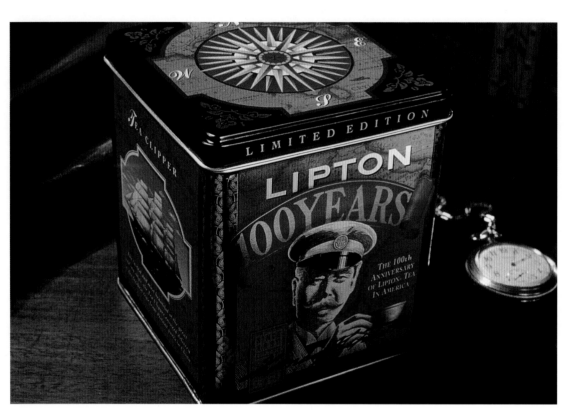

Lipton Tea 100th Anniversary Commemorative Tin

The design objective for this commemorative tea tin was to reflect a historical image that would appeal to contemporary tastes. We sought to represent the tradition of quality established by Sir Thomas J. Lipton by combining illustration and design motifs that simulate the effect of 19th-century steel-point engravings. Of the large number of these limited-edition commemorative tea tins that were produced, I signed only 300. Pam Clark and Ted Labiner coordinated the full integration of this assignment throughout the anniversary campaign.

Dogbolter Beer

The design assignment was to build a brand identity for Dogbolter that would be seen
as traditional, established, masculine, and special but not trendy. The solution: a unique
label-shape in two colors, printed directly on the glass bottle. Simple, strong typography
supports and reinforces Dogbolter's image.

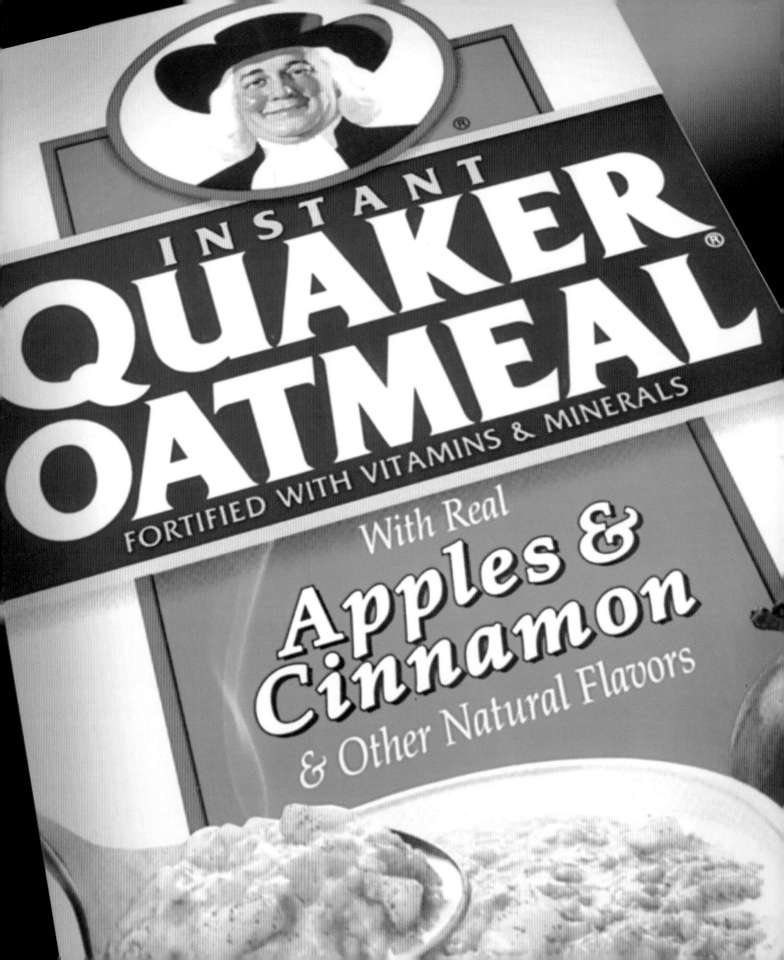

Quaker Oats

In redesigning the hot cereal packaging for Quaker Oats, PAI's objectives were to boost shelf impact, improve taste appeal, and contemporize the package without compromising existing equities. We first eliminated the competition between brand and product identifiers by enlarging the Quaker icon and expanding the area of the new, bolder branding bar; we then incorporated typographic values to reverse out the type on the branding bar, reduce the word "Instant," and soften the type of the product identifier. To enhance taste appeal, on some varieties we added the image of a piping-hot spoonful of cereal coming toward the viewer, with a line of steam wafting into the product identifier panel to draw the eye upward to the brand. On other varieties we included appetizing photographic images of the fruits and spices represented in the different flavors. Through these adjustments, the new Quaker Oats packaging heightens branding and taste appeal while preserving the impact of the brand's respected heritage.

Zima

With George Chadwick of client agency Foote, Cone & Belding in San Francisco, PAI developed this concept to capture the clean, refreshing, cutting-edge personality of Coors' uniquely flavored new malt beverage, Zima. Lightly carbonated but crystal clear, this naturally flavored drink offers consumers an alternative to traditional alcohol beverages. At a later date, Libby Perszyk Kathman of Cincinnati joined the design team to complete the bottle structure component of the project. After several months in successful test markets, Zima has been rolled out into broad-based distribution across the United States.

137

Oakland A's 1987
All-Star Game Uniforms

The new uniforms for the Oakland Athletics play on the tradition of the Athletics ball club, the oldest team in the American League. The earlier, multicolor uniforms, commissioned by former owner Charlie Finley, looked like show business costumes; we replaced them with a more traditional-looking uniform featuring the Athletics logo and, on the sleeve, the symbol we created to commemorate the 1987 All-Star Game, played in Oakland. We used the letter A of the Athletics logo to form the revolving blue-and-red star. Following the uniform redesign, the Athletics went to the World Series three successive years in a row. Coincidence?

Seattle's Best Coffee

This famous Seattle coffee merchant approached us to develop new packaging graphics that retain SBC's heritage, enhance the brand's place among other premium coffees, and project a consistent and highly identifiable message to consumers. We used rich colors and vivid, aromatic imagery to capture the spirit and quality of this fine coffee.

Harp Lager

A few words from Brian Reid, Guinness Brand Manager: "Harp is the only indigenous Irish lager brand; its very Irishness became its problem. Young Irish drinkers wanted the 'fast international buzz' of Budweiser and Carlsberg. They rationalized their move away from Harp by alleging poor product and a dated image. The livery revamp [package redesign] was a key element in turning double-digit decline into moderate growth – all in the space of one year. The brand manager lived to fight another day."

Veryfine Chillers

*Al Carosi, Vice President of Marketing at Veryfine Products Inc.,
assigned us the task of incorporating the new Veryfine brand
identity as an endorsement into the Chillers line. The key order
was to improve the branding and develop a cooler, more refreshing
personality. The privilege of working directly with Veryfine's
President, Sam Rowse, gave us a leg up when designing this
twelve-flavored line.*

Primo Angeli Inc. Web Site

PAI evolved naturally and full force into Web site design for the Internet. It was a comfortable progression that grew out of our effectiveness in branding, packaging, and print work and our complete immersion and considerable investment in high-tech equipment. It is natural for product or service companies to turn to brand and package designers to build their Web sites. We are used to getting our message across in small spaces. The Web page has to have the simplicity and impact of packaging and yet it must be informative and emotionally charged. The right mix of designer and technician does this exceptionally well if the dedication is to communication rather than technique.
The PAI Web site is http://www.primo.com

Index

1550 Bryant Street, 131
500th Anniversary
 of Columbus's Discovery of
 America, poster project for, 84

Ackerman, Diane, *A Natural
 History of the Senses*, 14
ACOG (Atlanta Committee for
 the Olympic Games), 109
Adobe software, 14, 85
Adobe Illustrator
 (graphics software), 103
advertising, 6, 27, 95;
 and packaging design, 18;
 television, 28
aesthetic concerns, 7, 10
All-Star Game, 1987
 (Oakland), 138
Almond Roca, 40, 43
American League, 138
Andelin, Jerry
 (of Hal Riney & Partners), 8
Angeli, Primo, 10
Anheuser-Busch, 28
Apple (computers), 14
Arrowhead (logotype), 133
art, 6, 7; commercial, 6, 112;
 fine, 11
artist, 6, 8; commercial, 7
Asian Art Museum
 (logotype), 132
architecture, design of
 environmental graphics in
 conjunction with, 60, 62,
 64, 67, 68, 71, 72
Atec (logotype), 132
Atlanta (Georgia), 68,
 104-106, 108-110
Atlanta Committee for the
 Olympic Games (ACOG), 104
authorship, sharing, 12

Bagley, Mark (marketing
 director, Mariani Packing
 Company), 22, 27
beer, 13;
 packaging redesign, 28-33
BeerGear (logotype), 123
Berkeley (California), 63
biscotti (Just Desserts),
 example of RapidAccess®,
 94-98
Boudin, 114; poster, 76
brand, 13; equity, capitalize on,
 41; mark, easily identifiable,
 48; name, divided from
 product name, 31
BrewMakers, 123
Brown & Haley, redesign of
 brand identity, 40-43
Budweiser (company), 139
Burdett, Susan, director of
 creative development, Miller
 Brewing Company, 120

Business Horizons, 92
Butterfinger, 38, 39, 118
buyer (consumer), potential, 11

Cambridge Plan, 115
Carlsberg (company), 139
Carosi, Al (vice president in
 charge of marketing,
 Veryfine Products Inc.), 140
Carson, David (designer), 17
Cerletti, Larry,
 of Lucca Delis, 122
Clark, Pam, 134
client(s), 8, 16, 36, 37;
 designer's obligations to, 7;
 in relation to the design process,
 102; standpoint of, 10
Chadwick, George, of Foote,
 Cone and Belding, 137
Cheskin, Louis, 90
chocolate(s), 13, 38, 44-46;
 colors used for packaging of, 15
color schemes, in environmental
 graphics, 71, 72
communication, 10, 11, 13,
 14, 16-18, 141 (*see also*
 visual communication);
 business of, 112; emotional
 level of marketing, 11;
 marketing, 10; products 28;
 with customer, 28
compatibility (between
 packaging and product), 13
comps, definition of, 89
comps and roughs, package, 25
computer systems, designing
 packaging for applications
 for, 48-53; managers,
 designing packaging to
 appeal to, 48
confections, designing
 packages for, 38-46
consumer(s), 5, 7, 11-13, 15,
 22, 25, 32, 36; American,
 10; anticipation by, of the
 product, 14; expectations
 of, 11; place in the design
 process, 89, 90; testing,
 limitations of, 90;
 transference of C.'s sensations
 from package to product, 91
Coors, 137
Copeland, Brad (of Copeland
 Hirthler/Murrell), 105
Copeland Hirthler/Murrell
 (Atlanta), 105, 109
creative process, 8, 12
creative teams,
 composition of, 12
Crystal Geyser (logotype), 132
cummings, e. e. (quotation), 80
cyberspace, 17

DCT (logotype), 133
Del Monte, 22;
 Pasta Sauces, 113
design(s), 11-13, 15, 18, 31;

beer label, 32; concepts,
 abandoning of, 12; for a
 captive audience, 54-58;
 group, 8; package, 28;
 philosophy, 8; signage, 60;
 structure, evaluation of
 concepts, 57; typographic
 (example), 46
designing, "out of the box,"
 88, 92; to develop brand
 equity, 127
designer(s), 5, 11, 14, 15, 18,
 20; communications and
 marketing, 21; marketing,
 not using a personal style, 112;
 the most valuable asset of, 12
Design Five (Atlanta Olympics
 design group), 107, 109
DHL Worldwide Express
 (logotype), 132
Diefenbach, John,
 director of San Francisco
 Film Society, 100
dissonance (communications), 13
Dogbolter Beer, 135
Dole, 22
dried-fruit, designing
 packaging for, 20-27
Dulbecco, Melanie, of R. Torre
 and Company, 118

emotion(s), 16, 18
environmental graphic design,
 59-72
environmental graphics,
 definition, 60, 61
Esprit, 131
evolutionary design change,
 28, 39
ethnic name, effectiveness of,
 in branding, 122
Evans, Robert
 (air-brush artist), 26

Fantastic Foods (logotype), 133
Favermann Design (Boston),
 105, 109
Favermann, Mark
 (of Favermann Design), 105
Feinstein, Dianne, 84
Ferrari, Paul, of Lucca
 Delicatessen, Inc., 122
Ferris & Roberts, 116, 117
Festa Italiana 85, 79
Festa Italiana, poster for, 78
filmmakers, 6
Finley, Charlie, former owner
 of Oakland A's, 138
focus group, 7, 30, 36, 89
Foote, Cone and Belding
 (advertising agency), 137
Ford, 48
foreign-language and -market
 specialists, 17
"frequent repeat purchase,"
 11, 88; products, 48
G. Heileman Brewing

Company, 32, 35
Galli, David, communications
 director at XILINX, 49
Giorgi, Peter, president,
 P.G. Molinari & Sons, 124
Glickman, Ruben (attorney), 124
GlobalCenter, 141
global market, 11
Godiva (chocolates), 14, 44
Gold Coast (lager), 124
Golden Gate Bridge, 86;
 50th anniversary poster, 82
graphic designer(s), 6, 10
 (*see also* designer(s))
graphics, 10, 11, 18, 39;
 packaging, honest
 representation of product,
 38; typography as, 17
Grace Cathedral
 (San Francisco), 85
Grear, Malcolm, of Malcolm
 Grear Designers Inc., 109
Grid, 133
Guinness, 120, 139

Hair, poster for, 75
Hamm's Brewery, 131;
 building brochure, 131
Hanzlovic, Jack
 (of G. Heileman Brewing
 Company), 35
Harden & Huyse (chocolates),
 14; packaging design,
 44-46
Hardenne, Anthony and Claude
 (of Harden & Huyse), 44
Harp (lager), 139
Harris, Oscar (of Turner and
 Associates), 105, 109
Heileman's Old Style beer,
 redesign of, 28-31;
 Premium Dry, 28-31;
 Premium Light, 28-31
Henry Weinhard's, 8;
 Private Reserve Beer, Light,
 Dark, redesign of, 32, 33;
 Root Beer, 90; graphics and
 structural design, 34-37
heritage, power of, 30; use of,
 in packaging design, 142
Hills Brothers, Plaza Building,
 design of environmental
 graphics for, 62
Hills Brothers Coffee, Inc., 62
Hine, Thomas,
 The Total Package, 90, 91
Howard, Dr. Alan (originator
 of Cambridge Plan), 115
Hyatt Hotels, designing
 customer amenities for, 54-57

ice-cream toppings
 (Just Desserts), 98
identity, graphic, 22; product, 39
industrial designers, 6
integration (of package
 and product), 14
international (marketing)

regions, 17
Internet, 127, 141
intuition, 7, 15, 16
intuitive feeling, 13

Japanese packaging, 20, 27
John Portman & Associates
 (architectural designers), 68
Jones, Alan, Very Reverend
 Dean (Grace Cathedral,
 San Francisco), 85
Jones Worley Design (Atlanta),
 105, 109
Just Desserts, package design
 for RapidAccess® product,
 92-98

Kathman, Libby Perszyk
 (designer), 137
Kornick Lindsay,
 structural design firm, 142

Labiner, Ted, 134
Lavazza (logotype), 133
Lindt (chocolates), 44
line extension(s), 32, 35, 88
Lipton Tea
 (100th Anniversary Tin), 134
"literal branding," 28
logotype(s), 25, 26, 138;
 design of, 43, 46;
 enhancement of, 70;
 use of in point-of-sale
 items, 103
Lucca Delicatessen, Inc., 122;
 (logotype) 132
Lucheta, Lisa,
 of R. Torre and Company,
 118; Paula, 118

Mariani, Mark
 (owner, Mariani Packing
 Company), 22, 27
Mariani Packing Company,
 repackaging of dried-fruit
 line, 20-27; redesigning
 the brand mark for, 23
marketer, 11, 12, 14, 15
marketing, 7, 10, 12;
 design, 5, 12; on-line, 18;
 research, 15
materials (as used in
 packaging), 13, 14, 49
McMacken, David
 (mural artist), 67
Metro (fragrance), 129
Michels, Kate, creative
 director of marketing
 services for Visa USA, 131
Miller Brewing Company,
 28, 120
Milpitas, 127
Mission Dolores,
 poster celebrating, 85
mixed signals,
 designed into a message, 13
name generation, 16

natural materials
   (use in packaging), 20
Nescafe Espresso, 119
Nestlé, 14, 39
Nestlé USA, 118
Nestlé, Carnation Coffee-mate,
   119; Carnation Milk Chocolate,
   119; Cosmo, 119; Libby's,
   Asian Favorites, 119;
   Nestea, 119; Quik, 119
new-product development, 88-92
New York Package Designers
   Council, 124
Noah's Bagels (logotype), 132

Oakland Athletics
   (baseball team), 138
Oka, Hideyuki,
   How to Wrap Five Eggs, 20
Olympic Games, designing the
   "look" of, 10, 104-110
Olympics, Visa, project for, 131
Omnihost, 52, 53
"orange crate graphics," 26
Ortega, Robert
   (photographer/designer), 96
Orville Redenbacher's, 133
overpackaging, 10, 14, 19

P.G. Molinari & Sons, poster,
   81; salame cannister, 124
Pabst, 32
Pacific Dry, 124
packaging, 10-13, 18, 20, 36;
   design of, 7; designers, 8;
   of food, 15; transference of
   sensation from, to product, 91;
   use of dynamic graphics in, 53
Paramount, 128
Payne, William Porter
   (president and CEO of the
   Atlanta Olympic Committee
   for the Olympic Games), 106
Pendás, Miguel (publication
   officer, San Francisco Film
   Society), 100
Pendleton Woolen Mills, 85
Pete's Brewing Company, 124
Pete's Wicked Ale, 125
pictograms, 102, 131; for the
   Atlanta Olympics, 109
Pixel Paint Professional, 126
positioning, brand, 30;
   product, 38
posters, designing, 74
Primo Angeli Inc., 127, 137,
   141; design philosophy,
   strength of, 112; the firm's
   work, 8; Web page, 141;
   Web site, 141
product(s), 8, 11, 12, 14, 16, 17,
   20, 26, 27, 36; categories,
   27; design, 88-92; failure
   rate of, 88, 92; food, 12, 14;
   food (as subject for marketing
   design), 27; graphics, 39;
   identifier, 30; names, 16;

non-shelf-competitive, 47-58,
   115; performance, 22; selling a,
   10; transference of sensation
   from packaging to, 91
prototypes, use of,
   in market testing, 90

Qantas, 83
Quaker Oats (company), 10,
   137; Oatmeal, 133, 136
Quantum Corporation,
   127, 133; Web page, 141
"quilt" motif
   (in Atlanta Olympics),
   as umbrella design, 107

R.J. Nabisco, 39
R. Torre and Company,
   management and marketing
   team, 118
RapidAccess®, 87-98
Ray Gun magazine, 17
Reid, Brian (brand manager,
   Guinness), 139
research, and development
   (of products) in relation to
   designing, 91; marketing-
   research results and design
   options, 36
Riney, Hal (chief executive
   officer and chairman,
   Hal Riney & Partners,
   San Francisco), 6, 8, 32, 33
Rowse, Sam (president,
   Veryfine Products Inc.), 140

Samaranch, Juan Antonio,
   International Olympics
   Committee President, 110
San Francisco Fashion Center, 68
San Francisco Film Society,
   identity for, 100
San Francisco International
   Airport (poster), 77
San Francisco International
   Film Festival, 81;
   38th Annual, traditional
   design, 100-103
San Francisco Symphony, 84
Sarks, 119
Saskatchewan, 44

Scarlet, Peter
   (president of San Francisco
   Film Society), 100
scent(s), 14; as visual element
   in package graphics, 15
Seattle's Best Coffee, 139
"sensation transference,"
   theory of, 90
sense appeal, 14-17
senses, 14-16; sensory level
   of communication, 11
service(s), 12; selling a, 10
Shaklee, 129
Sharp's (Miller), 120, 121
"shelf-competitive" items

(products), 88
"shelf-competitive products,"
   118; designing packaging for,
   19-46; wholesale market, 96
shopping center(s), 12, 53;
   virtual, 18
signage, design of,
   62, 63, 65-68, 70-72;
   use of interchangeables, 72
"The Silent Majority" (poster), 75
Simpson Paper (poster), 80
software packaging, 48-53
Spectrum Foods, 116
Speyers, Lars (photographer), 75
Stanford Design Conference,
   1982, 96
stationery, application of
   trademark to, 101
structure design
   (for packaging), 27
Sunset (magazine; logotype), 132
Sunsweet, 22
SUPERMAC Graphics Card, 126
SUPERMAC Technology
   (logotype), 132
Swig, Charlotte Mailliard,
   San Francisco, 86
symbols, use of,
   in packaging design, 51, 53

taste appeal, 11, 12;
   (in graphics) 26
temperature, as visual element
   in package graphics, 11, 15
texture, 11, 16, 26
Tompkins, Susie, of Esprit, 131
Torani, 118
trademark, characteristics of
   a great, 100; redesign of, 43
TransAmerica building, 83
TreeSweet (logotype), 133
Turner Associates (architectural
   firm, Atlanta), 105
Tutto Mare, 116
Twain, Mark (Samuel Clemens), 16

Verifone, Inc., 53
Veryfine (logotype), 132
Veryfine Products Inc., 140
Visa USA, 131
Visa, 130
visual communication, basic
   principles, 10; identity, 53;
   impact, 10; language, 10;
   presentation, 31; signal, 36;
   styles, personal, 11; system,
   116; vocabulary, 67; visual
   presentation in secondary
   beer packaging, 31

Watkins, Ginger (managing
   director of corporate services
   of the Atlanta Committee for
   the Olympic Games), 105
WD-40 (aerosol lubricant), 103
Web site, 12; design of, 141
Winter Games (1992)

in Lillehammer, 109
words, as used in package
   design, 16, 17
World Series, 138
World Wide Web, 127
Worley, Barry (of Jones Worley
   Design, *which see*), 105
WPA (use of mural style),
   63, 67
writing, 16

XACT 4000,
   designing package for, 49, 50
XILINX
   (software manufacturer), 49

Zima, 137; (logotype), 132

Contributors

Designer
Roberto Carra

Editor
Daniel Imhoff

Cover Design
Primo Angeli

Cover Illustration
Mark Jones

Photography
Roberto Carra
June Fouché
Chun Y Lai
Rodger Macuch
Jaime Pandolfo

Copy Editor
Christopher Bernard

Project Coordination
John Eagle

Special Thanks to
Philippe Becker
Marcelo De Freitas
Jean Galeazzi
Cummings Walker

Printer
C & C Offset Printing Co., Ltd.

Bindery
C & C Offset Printing Co., Ltd.

Separations
C & C Offset Printing Co., Ltd.

Typography
Text: Bauer Bodoni
Cover: Gill Sans, Bauer Bodoni

Stock
135gsm Finnish Galerie
Glossy Art

Ink
Four-color process,
gloss and dull varnish

Software
QuarkXpress 3.32
Adobe Photoshop 3.51
Adobe Illustrator 6.0
Microsoft Word 6.0
Suitcase 3.0
System 7.5

Work Stations
Apple Power Macintosh 8500 /
150Mhz / 256MB / 2.0GB /
4XCD / 4GBExternal /
21" Magnavox / 4MBVRAM /
Power User 24-bit Video Board

Apple Power Macintosh 7600 /
120Mhz / 80MB / 2.0GB /
4XCD / 2GBExternal /
21" Magnavox / 2MBVRAM

Scanner
Agfa Arcus II

Printers
Tektronix Phaser 480
Hewlett Packard LaserJet 4MV